9/12

D0036623

WALKING
ROME

WALKING

ROME

THE BEST OF THE CITY

Katie Parla

NATIONAL GEOGRAPHIC

Washington, D.C.

WALKING ROME

CONTENTS

PART 1

PAGE 12
WHIRLWIND TOURS

PART 2

PAGE 36
ROME'S NEIGHBORHOODS

PART 3

PAGE 174
TRAVEL ESSENTIALS

Previous pages: Piazza Navona; left: Fontana di Nettuno in Piazza Navona; right: Temple of Castor and Pollux; above right, the Spanish Steps; bottom right, Roman ice cream selection

Introduction

I came to Rome late in life. I'd visited its great Italian brethren many times—Florence, Capri, Venice. Somehow, Rome didn't make it onto my dance card. Rome challenges you to give up the extravagances of the modern—digital games, GPS directives, cell phones—and time-travel back to grasp how astonishingly inventive we humans were before electricity and how brilliant the Roman artists, architects, and engineers were so long ago. On a humid Saturday blessed by sun-scattering clouds, I walked Rome's streets with an art expert. She slipped me in and out of small museums, private gardens, and pocket parks. She stroked the centuries-old stone face of the Colosseo as she described gladiatorial battles held before as many as 60,000 spectators.

Renaissance master Botticelli frescoed the walls of the Sistine Chapel with scenes depicting the Old Testament prophet Moses.

Rome is really two cities. The first is the great, sprawling early engine of the civilized world—2,500 years old and the bastion of the warrior Caesars. This is the Rome my companion showed me. But tucked into that urban host is Vatican City—actually, the world's smallest state, with its own stamps and currency. Here she took me to museums brimming with world-class art from the greats—Raphael and Botticelli, Rodin and Dalí. We beheld the Sistine Chapel, with Michelangelo's glorious frescoes. Without my guide, I would have missed so much. She gave me insights, delighted in obscurities, and steered me right. This book will do the same for you.

Keith Bellows

Editor-in-Chief, National Geographic Traveler *magazine*

Visiting Rome

With a rambling layout that reflects its long and varied history, five million visitors a year, and streets filled with cars and scooters, Rome can present a noisy and chaotic aspect to newcomers. But its quiet corners will reward the intrepid.

Rome in a Nutshell

Rome was born on a number of hills and their intervening valleys around the sixth century B.C. (though legend would place the foundation earlier, in 753 B.C.). These areas remained the heart of the city until the Middle Ages, when life shifted to the flood plain due north. Today, both areas are populated with apartment buildings, churches, shopping districts, and cultural attractions. On the opposite side of the Tiber River (il Tevere) lie Trastevere, the Vatican, and sprawling residential zones.

Navigating Rome

The city's complex layout coupled with (often) inadequate maps can make navigating Rome a frustrating prospect. Street names change from

Rome Day-by-Day

Open every day The Foro Romano, Colosseo, Palatino, and Terme di Caracalla (Baths of Caracalla).

Monday Most state- and city-run sites are closed, except for the above. The Musei Vaticani and privately run attractions, including the Case Romane al Celio, San Clemente, and the Villa Farnesina, are open.

Tuesday All sites are open, except the Case Romane al Celio and the Vicus Caprarius.

Wednesday All sites are open, except the Case Romane al Celio.

Thursday All sites are open. San Luigi dei Francesi is closed in the afternoon.

Friday All sites open. The Museo Ebraico closes in the late afternoon for Shabbat.

Saturday The Museo Ebraico and other Jewish sites in the Ghetto are closed for Shabbat. All other sites are open.

Sunday Most museums and sites remain open on Sundays, except the Musei Vaticani (open last Sunday of the month until 12:30 p.m.) and the Villa Farnesina. San Clemente opens at noon.

Dining alfresco in a lovely cobbled side street after a hard day's sightseeing is one of the many pleasures the city offers visitors.

one block to the next, roads twist and turn, and signage is often limited. But getting lost is part of the fun, and sticking to main roads means missing out on Rome's undeniable beauty. For a comprehensive and accurate navigational guide, pick up a *Stradario,* a spiral-bound book of maps on sale at newsstands. You will find maps of the city and its transport displayed at Metro stations, many of which have an attendant who can answer basic questions. When exploring Trastevere or the Campo Marzio (Field of Mars), don't rely on the Tiber for orientation.

Most of central Rome is on the left bank; Trastevere and the Vatican are on the right. The river twists and turns so much that it is not reliable for direction.

Enjoying Rome for Less

Admission fees in Rome tend to be high, particularly for special exhibitions. Purchase a Roma Pass *(www.romapass .it)* to get free admission to two sites, discounted admission to others, and a three-day transit pass. *La Settimana della Cultura* (Culture Week) in spring and other initiatives through the year allow free entry to state-run museums and archaeological sites.

Using This Guide

Each tour—which might be only a walk, or might take advantage of the city's public transportation as well—is plotted on a map and has been planned to take into account opening hours and the times of day when sites are less crowded. Many end near restaurants or lively night spots for evening activities.

Whirlwind Tours

Whirlwind Tours are for people who have only a day or a weekend to spend in the city and want to be sure that they see the best of the best. Choose your tour based on your time and interests: One Day; Weekend (Day 1 & Day 2); For Fun; and With Kids (Day 1 & Day 2).

Tips For the Day and Weekend Tours, a Tips spread following the itinerary map provides insider information on detours from the key sites, extra places to see, nearby cafés and restaurants, and ideas for adapting the tours to suit your interests.

Site Descriptions
In the For Fun and With Kids tours, key sites spreads following the maps provide descriptions of all the sites and practical information for visitors.

Neighborhood Tours

The nine neighborhood tours each begin with an introduction, followed by an itinerary map highlighting the key sites that make up the tour and detailed key sites descriptions. Each tour is followed by an "in-depth" spread showcasing one major site along the route, a "distinctly" Rome spread providing background information on a quintessential element of that neighborhood, and a "best of" spread that groups sites thematically.

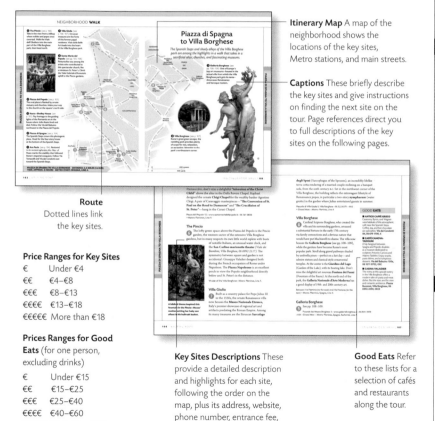

Itinerary Map A map of the neighborhood shows the locations of the key sites, Metro stations, and main streets.

Captions These briefly describe the key sites and give instructions on finding the next site on the tour. Page references direct you to full descriptions of the key sites on the following pages.

Route Dotted lines link the key sites.

Price Ranges for Key Sites

€	Under €4
€€	€4–€8
€€€	€8–€13
€€€€	€13–€18
€€€€€	More than €18

Prices Ranges for Good Eats (for one person, excluding drinks)

€	Under €15
€€	€15–€25
€€€	€25–€40
€€€€	€40–€60
€€€€€	More than €60

Key Sites Descriptions These provide a detailed description and highlights for each site, following the order on the map, plus its address, website, phone number, entrance fee, days closed, and nearest Metro station and bus stops.

Good Eats Refer to these lists for a selection of cafés and restaurants along the tour.

PART 1

Whirlwind Tours

Rome in a Day

Ramble around ancient sites, savor the awe-inspiring atmosphere of San Pietro, and mingle with street life in Rome's festive squares.

8 Basilica di San Pietro

(see pp. 135–136) **Visit Bernini's** sweeping piazza and the most important pilgrimage site in Rome. Head to the environs of the Fontana di Trevi by taking the 62 bus to Via del Corso, or the Metro Line A from Ottaviano to Barberini.

7 Campo de' Fiori (see p. 121)
This Renaissance square hosts a produce market in the morning and accommodates outdoor cafés all day and evening. Backtrack two blocks to Corso Vittorio Emanuele II and take the 62 bus four stops to San Pietro.

6 Piazza Navona
(see p. 123) **The elegant** baroque square was built on the footprint of an ancient stadium, which accounts for its elongated shape. Walk three blocks south to Campo de' Fiori.

5 Pantheon
(see pp. 124–125) Contemplate the engineering of the ancients beneath the Pantheon's solid concrete dome. Walk a few blocks west to Piazza Navona.

ROME IN A DAY   DISTANCE: 5.8 MILES (9.3 KM)
TIME: APPROX. 9 HOURS   METRO START: COLOSSEO, LINE B

9 Fontana di Trevi (see p. 92)
The light and atmosphere around the Trevi Fountain are unforgettable after sunset—as is the nighttime view of the city from the top of the Spanish Steps.

1 Colosseo (see pp. 66–67)
Wander through the corridors of Rome's most iconic building, where emperors wooed the masses with their extravagant public spectacles. Stroll along Via dei Fori Imperiali 750 feet (229 m) northwest to the Foro Romano entrance.

WHIRLWIND TOURS

4 Musei Capitolini (see p. 46)
Peruse the unrivaled collection of ancient statues in one of the world's oldest museums. Descend to Piazza Venezia, head west to Largo di Torre Argentina, and take Via de' Cestari to the Pantheon.

3 Piazza del Campidoglio (see p. 45) Michelangelo designed the elegant square, which many consider Rome's most beautiful, and the ornate surrounding palaces. Enter the Musei Capitolini from the western side of the square.

2 Foro Romano (see pp. 50–51)
Explore the surviving monuments in the ancient city center. The Romans commanded their empire from government, legal, and religious buildings located here. Exit at the northwestern end, and climb the staircase to the top of the Capitolino.

Tips

These are the best of the best Roman sights. All are described elsewhere in the book—just follow the cross-references for more detailed information. These tips provide advice on visiting these major locations when you have limited time and also suggest additional sights nearby and places to eat.

❶ Colosseo (see pp. 66–67) For another peek at the past, visit the ■ UNDERGROUND SIGHTS beneath the nearby church of San Clemente (see pp. 63–64). The lowest level was built around A.D. 80. Also nearby are the ■ CASE ROMANE AL CELIO, two ancient Roman houses buried below the church of Santi Giovanni e Paolo (see pp. 60–62).

Pieces of a huge statue of Emperor Constantine lie at the entrance to the Musei Capitolini.

❷ Foro Romano (see pp. 50–51) On sunny summer days, head to the southern side of the ■ BASILICA OF JULIUS CAESAR (south side of the Forum), where you can sit on ancient stones in the shade of pine trees away from the crowds at the center of the Forum.

❸ Piazza del Campidoglio (see p. 45) If the chaos and heat of the forum become unbearable, pop into the medieval church of ■ SANTA MARIA IN ARACOELI (see pp. 46–47), a surprisingly cool and tranquil retreat on the peak of the Capitolino. Don't miss the sweeping views from the ■ TOP OF THE STAIRCASE rising from the Foro Romano.

❹ Musei Capitolini (see p. 46) If you have time, descend the Capitolino to the church of ■ SAN NICOLA IN CARCERE (*Via del Teatro di Marcello 46*). Beneath it lie the ruins of three republican-era temples, for which guided tours are available. Likewise if time allows, you can visit Rome's signature 19th-century landmark below the forum, the ■ VITTORIANO (*Piazza Venezia*), and take in its Risorgimento museum and panoramic terrace on the roof. Have a quick bite in the ■ CAFFÈ CAPITOLINO (*Piazzale Caffarelli*), accessible from the museum, which offers splendid views over Rome from the terrace. For a more lingering lunch, head to ■ LA TAVERNA DEGLI AMICI (*Piazza Tormargana 37*) for traditional Roman fare on your way to the Pantheon, or try the family-run ■ ARMANDO AL PANTHEON, 150 yards (137 m) east of the building itself.

❺ Pantheon (see pp. 124–125) In addition to its stellar beauty, the Pantheon has two great advantages: There are never lines to get in and admission is free. If your visit coincides with the hours of Saturday or Sunday Mass, when it is closed to tourists, kill some time grabbing a coffee at nearby ■ TAZZA D'ORO (*Via degli Orfani 84*), founded in 1946.

❻ Piazza Navona (see p. 123) Avoid the cafés on the square, which may charge up to five times the price of a coffee if you sit down rather than stand at the bar. ■ BRASCAFÉ in Palazzo Braschi at the south end of the square makes up in value what it loses in views.

SAVVY TRAVELER

Rome is a shopping capital, with small, locally owned boutiques populating the Monti and Trastevere districts and the streets around Piazza Navona. Luxury goods abound on Via dei Condotti, where all the major Italian designers have showrooms. There are big sales twice annually, in July–August and late December–January.

❼ Campo de' Fiori (see p. 121) This square is perhaps the best place in Rome for ■ PEOPLE-WATCHING, especially in late afternoon after the market has packed up and the area has been cleaned.

❽ Basilica di San Pietro (see pp. 135–136) By 5 p.m., the crowds in and around the Vatican diminish and Masses begin—a good moment for people with limited time to visit. Whether you care to worship or not, the sound of the ■ ORGAN AND CHOIR at this time of day is transcendent.

❾ Fontana di Trevi (see p. 92) Dine at ■ AL MORO (*Vicolo delle Bollette 13*) or ■ COLLINE EMILIANE (*Via degli Avignonesi 22*), then walk the few steps to the Trevi Fountain—it's quieter at night. Afterward, climb up the ■ SPANISH STEPS (see p. 104) or take the ■ ELEVATOR at the end of Vicolo del Bottino, next to the Metro.

Rome in a Weekend

Visit one of the city's richest museums, three of its iconic sites, Renaissance chapels, high-end designer shops, and two lively squares.

WHIRLWIND TOURS

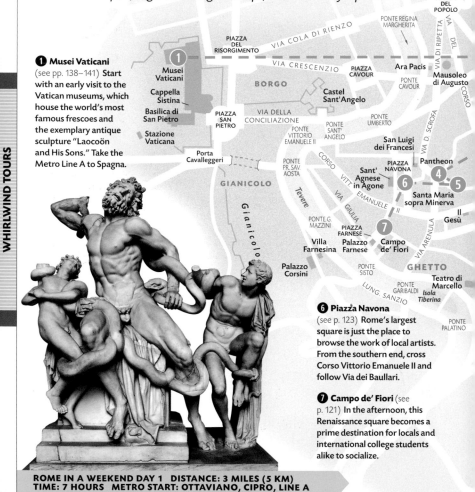

❶ Musei Vaticani (see pp. 138–141) **Start with an early visit to the Vatican museums, which house the world's most famous frescoes and the exemplary antique sculpture "Laocoön and His Sons." Take the Metro Line A to Spagna.**

❻ Piazza Navona (see p. 123) **Rome's largest square is just the place to browse the work of local artists. From the southern end, cross Corso Vittorio Emanuele II and follow Via dei Baullari.**

❼ Campo de' Fiori (see p. 121) **In the afternoon, this Renaissance square becomes a prime destination for locals and international college students alike to socialize.**

ROME IN A WEEKEND DAY 1 DISTANCE: 3 MILES (5 KM)
TIME: 7 HOURS METRO START: OTTAVIANO, CIPRO, LINE A

2 Piazza di Spagna (see p. 104) Admire Rome's most famous staircase and wander the streets below, around Via dei Condotti, where Europe's rich and famous shop (see pp. 98–99). Take Via Due Macelli southeast to Via del Tritone, turn right, then left at Via Poli.

0   1 kilometer
0             $\frac{1}{2}$ mile

3 Fontana di Trevi (see p. 92) Contemplate the ebullient statuary of Rome's signature fountain. Take Via delle Muratte west, cross Via del Corso, and continue through Via di Pietra.

4 Pantheon (see pp. 124–125) Marvel at ancient Rome's engineering prowess and visit the tomb of the Renaissance master, Raphael. Behind the building is Piazza della Minerva.

5 Santa Maria sopra Minerva (see p. 118) A plain facade hides opulent chapels containing the tombs of Rome's elite and art treasures such as Filippino Lippi's exquisite frescoes. Take Via Santa Chiara toward the historic café, Sant'Eustachio, and follow Via degli Staderari to Corso del Rinascimento.

Map labels:

Piazza Spagna
VIA DUE MACELLI
VIA DEL TRITONE
VIA DEI CONDOTTI
Santa Maria della Vittoria
Palazzo Barberini
Santa Maria degli Angeli
PIAZZA DELLA REPUBBLICA
Fontana di Trevi
Quirinale
San Carlo alle Quattro Fontane
Repubblica
PIAZZA DEI CINQUECENTO
Palazzo del Quirinale
VIA DEL QUIRINALE
Sant'Andrea al Quirinale
Museo Nazionale Romano
Termini
Stazione Termini
Pal. Doria Pamphili
Palazzo Colonna
VIA NAZIONALE
Viminale
PIAZZA DELL'ESQUILINO
Santa Maria Maggiore
PIAZZA VENEZIA
Mon. a Vitt. Emanuele II
Fori Imperiali
VIA CAVOUR
Cavour
VIA G. LANZA
PIAZZA VITTORIO EMANUELE II
VIA DEI FORI IMPERIALI
San Pietro in Vincoli
Vittorio Emanuele
Musei Capitolini
Capitolino
Esquilino
VIA MERULANA
Foro Romano
Colosseo
PARCO DI TRAIANO
Domus Aurea
VIA LABICANA
San Clemente

WHIRLWIND TOURS

Rome in a Weekend

Discover the Jewish quarter, ancient entertainment venues, two gorgeous medieval churches, and the center of modern Rome.

9 Piazza Venezia (see p. 120)
The heart of modern Rome, gateway to its ruins and baroque center, is dominated by a massive white marble monument celebrating Italy's late 19th-century unification.

8 Piazza del Campidoglio (see p. 45)
Michelangelo's 16th-century square turns its back on ancient Rome and faces the new Rome of the popes. Descend the low-grade staircase, and follow the sidewalk right into busy Piazza Venezia.

WHIRLWIND TOURS

CORSO VITT. EMANUELE II
VIA GIULIA

Sant' Agnese in Agone
PIAZZA NAVONA
Pantheon
LARGO DI TORRE ARGENTINA
PIAZZA / CAMPO DE' FIORI

Santa Maria sopra Minerva
Pal. Doria Pamphili
Palazzo Colonna
Il Gesù
PIAZZA VENEZIA
Mon. a Vitt. Emanuele II
9

PONTE G. MAZZINI
PIAZZA FARNESE
Villa Farnesina
Palazzo Farnese

Gianicolo

Palazzo Corsini

PONTE SISTO

Santa Maria in Trastevere

LUNG. SANZIO
PONTE GARIBALDI
Isola Tiberina

VIA DI SAN FRANCESCO A RIPA

Santa Cecilia in Trastevere
PONTE PALATINO

Ghetto
1

VIA ARENULA

Santa Maria in Aracoeli
PIAZZA DEL CAMPIDOGLIO
8
Musei Capitolini

Teatro di Marcello

Capitolino
7

Fori Imperiali
VIA DEI FORI IMPERIALI

Foro Romano

Palatino

Santa Maria in Cosmedin
2
Circo Massimo
3

Tevere

VIA DEI CERCHI
VIA DEL

Circo Massimo
Ⓜ

Aventino

VIA / VIALE AVENTINO
P. CESTIA

1 The Ghetto (see pp. 170–171) Bernini's tortoises adorn the fountain in Piazza Mattei, a highlight of the Ghetto. Walk through the Teatro di Marcello archaeological site, then south along Via del Teatro di Marcello and Via L. Petroselli.

2 Santa Maria in Cosmedin (see p. 166) This stunning medieval church displays the Bocca della Verità in its porch. Take Via della Greca one block southeast.

3 Circo Massimo (see pp. 166–167) Ancient Rome's largest venue hosted chariot races for 250,000 spectators. Exit near the southeastern end, and take Via delle Terme di Caracalla.

**ROME IN A WEEKEND DAY 2 DISTANCE: 5.5 MILES (8.8 KM)
TIME: 8.5 HOURS START: LARGO ARGENTINA, BUS: 40, 62, 64, 87**

6 Colosseo (see pp. 66–67) Free food and entertainment drew more than 50,000 at a time to Rome's largest amphitheater. Take Via dei Fori Imperiali, and turn left at the second stoplight.

7 Foro Romano (see pp. 50–51) Classical ruins mingle with medieval churches in Rome's ancient center. Exit at the northwest end, and climb the staircase to the top.

5 San Clemente (see pp. 63–64) Rome's urban history is revealed in two underground levels excavated beneath a 12th-century church. Follow Via di San Giovanni in Laterano three blocks west.

VIA NAZIONALE

Viminale

VIA CAVOUR

Santa Maria Maggiore

M Cavour
VIA G. LANZA

San Pietro in Vincoli

PARCO DI TRAIANO

Esquilino

PIAZZA VITTORIO EMANUELE II

Vittorio Emanuele M

M Colosseo
PIAZZA DEL COLOSSEO

Domus Aurea

Colosseo

VIA MERULANA

VIA

LABICANA

Manzoni M

6 rco i Costantino

5 San Clemente

VIA SAN GIOVANNI IN LATERANO

PIAZZA DI SAN GIOVANNI IN LATERANO

San Gregorio Magno

VIA CLAUDIA

VILLA CELIMONTANA

Celio

VIA NAVICELLA

VIAD. NAVICELLA

VIA DRUSO

VIA DELL'AMBA ARADAM

Porta Metronia

VIA DELLE TERME DI CARACALLA

4 Terme di Caracalla

0 ——— 1 kilometer
0 ——— ½ mile

4 Terme di Caracalla (see pp. 167–168) The ruins of this bathing complex are set in a quiet archaeological park. Backtrack to the Circo Massimo, and take the 3 tram to Via Labicana.

Tips

Rome's major sights can be seen in two days. Refer to the cross-references provided in each entry below for detailed information elsewhere in the book. There's also information here on detours to nearby sights and highlights, and local cafés and restaurants, as well as suggestions for customizing the tour to suit your own interests.

WHIRLWIND TOURS

DAY 1

❶ Musei Vaticani (see pp. 138–141) If you cover all you want at the Musei Vaticani in good time, make a short detour to ■ **Castel Sant'Angelo** (see pp. 136–137), and zone in on its upper floors. This former papal fortress turned palace is replete with Renaissance frescoes commissioned by the popes, and viewing is guaranteed to be a less crowded experience.

Bernini's elephant in Piazza della Minerva

❺ Santa Maria sopra Minerva (see p. 118) Stop in the piazza in front of the church to see Bernini's charming design for a ■ **BABY ELEPHANT** supporting a small obelisk (see pp. 84–85). The streets around the church, particularly Via Santa Caterina da Siena and Via dei Cestari, are known for their sacred vestments shops. The storefronts display intricately embroidered garments, as well as a dazzling array of chalices and liturgical instruments.

❼ Campo de' Fiori (see p. 121) For one of the best fish restaurants in Rome, try ■ **Il Sanlorenzo** (*Via dei Chiavari 4/5*), which serves great seafood dishes in a sophisticated setting; or visit familial and friendly ■ **Cantina Lucifero** (*Via del Pellegrino 53*), a small wine bar serving fondue, cheeses, and cured meats.

DAY 2

❶ The Ghetto (see pp. 170–171) In your wanderings, seek out the homey little storefront of ■ IL MONDO DI LAURA (*Via di Santa Maria de' Calderari 25, closed Fri. p.m. and Sat.)* for creative kosher cookies that are organic and dairy free. They are original to the pastrycook owner—some adapted from family recipes— and come in pretty packages that make ideal presents.

❷ Santa Maria in Cosmedin (see p. 166) The Bocca della Verità (Mouth of Truth) is the obvious attraction here, but also take time to view the ■ MEDIEVAL FRESCOES AND MOSAICS. This bastion of beauty also makes a cool retreat from the summer heat.

❸ Circo Massimo (see pp. 166–167) This large field draws joggers and dog walkers and is a lovely place for a ■ PICNIC. Grab a few savory treats and pastries from ■ CRISTALLI DI ZUCCHERO (*Via di San Teodoro 88)* at the northern end of the Circo Massimo. Or follow Via San Gregorio to the church of ■ SAN GIORGIO IN VELABRO (*Via del Velabro 19),* whose medieval tower rests on a third-century arch.

❹ San Clemente (see pp. 63–64) The small ■ GUIDEBOOK sold at the ticket office is a savvy investment and will certainly enlighten your path around the

CUSTOMIZING **YOUR DAY**

With at least one night in Rome, why not check out some of the city's best evening entertainments. Enjoy a jazz concert at Casa del Jazz, Big Mama, or Celiamontana Jazz, or visit the Opera, which moves to the dramatic outdoor venue of the Terme di Caracalla in summer. To find out what's going on, pick up a copy of *Roma C'é*, the weekly listings magazine.

complex and fascinating church and its underground levels. On Sunday mornings, visitors who wish to worship can attend ■ MASSES IN ENGLISH, but San Clemente does not open to sightseers until noon. In summer, ■ EVENING PERFORMANCES take place in the courtyard. Ask at the ticket office for details.

❾ Piazza Venezia (see p. 120) Pop into the ■ PALAZZO VENEZIA, the first major Renaissance palace in Rome. It was built by the Venetian pope Paul II and hosts traveling exhibitions. Head east past Colonna di Traiano to ■ AL VINO AL VINO (*Via dei Serpenti 19)* for wine and tasty Sicilian dishes like caponata (a cooked vegetable salad) and an assortment of savory tarts. Or meander to ■ CAFFÈ DORIA (*Via della Gatta 1A)* for grilled sandwiches, pastries, and a caffeinated pick-me-up.

WHIRLWIND TOURS

Rome for Fun

Enjoy art, delectable shops, and lovely views, then make for one of the city's most popular evening destinations.

❸ Chiostro del Bramante (see p. 26) Join the hip crowd at an art exhibition held within flawless Renaissance porticos. Zigzag east, crossing Via di Santa Maria dell'Anima.

❹ Piazza Navona (see pp. 26, 123) Stroll around the baroque square with its cooling fountains. Leave from the east side, cross Piazza San Eustachio, turning left, then right for Piazza della Rotonda.

❷ Via del Governo Vecchio (see pp. 26, 99) Shop like a pro among the exclusive and vintage boutiques on this street beloved by Romans. Rare finds will make unusually stylish souvenirs. Take Via di Parione to Arco della Pace.

❶ Campo de' Fiori (see pp. 26, 121) Start your morning with a creamy cappuccino and a pastry. Then tickle your senses at the aromatic produce market. From the north end of the square follow Via del Pellegrino, and turn right along Vicolo Savelli.

**ROME FOR FUN   DISTANCE: 4.5 MILES (7.2 KM)
TIME: APPROX. 8.5 HOURS   BUS START: 64, 492**

WHIRLWIND TOURS

VILLA BORGHESE

Porta Pinciana

VIALE DEL MURO TORTO

Pincio

⑧

Spagna Ⓜ

Scalinata della
Trinità dei Monti

Santa Maria
della Concezione

Barberini Ⓜ

VIA SISTINA

VIA CONDOTTI

VIA DUE MACELLI

⑦

Luxury
Shopping

VIA DEL TRITONE

PIAZZA
BARBERINI

Palazzo
Barberini

Quirinale

Fontana
di Trevi

Palazzo del
Quirinale

VIA DEL QUIRINALE

DEL CORSO

VIA V. VENETO

anta Maria
opra Minerva

Pal. Doria
Pamphilj

Il
esù

PIAZZA
VENEZIA

on. a Vitt.
manuele II

anta Maria
n Aracoeli

Musei
Capitolini

eatro di
Marcello

NTE
ATINO

Santa
Maria in
Cosmedin

⑩ **Trastevere** (see pp. 27, 146–152) The bus follows the Tiber River before dropping you at Piazza Trilussa, the gate into Trastevere. Stroll the lively neighborhood before picking a place for dinner.

⑧ **A Stroll to the Pincio** (see pp. 27, 102–103) At Piazza Trinità dei Monti, take a sweeping view of the city from the church. Enjoy the Villa Borghese gardens as you head northwest for more glorious views. Descend from the Pincio terrace.

⑨ **Ara Pacis** (see pp. 27, 104) Soak up the majestic beauty of Piazza del Popolo, then head south on Via di Ripetta for Ara Pacis, a monument honoring Emperor Augustus. Cross the river via Ponte Cavour, and take bus 280 from Piazza Cavour in the direction of Trastevere.

⑦ **Luxury Shopping** (see pp. 27, 98–99) Explore Piazza San Lorenzo in Lucina before stepping into the home of all top luxury brands, Via dei Condotti. At the north end, climb the Spanish Steps.

⑥ **Via di Campo Marzio** (see p. 27) Delve into the one-of-a-kind boutiques on this street. Walking north you reach Rome's upscale shopping areas.

⑤ **Pantheon** (see pp.26, 124–125) Admire this 2,000-year-old achievement of Roman civilization. Head north along Via della Maddalena to Santa Maria in Campo Marzio at the end.

Campo de' Fiori

1 This traditional and lively produce market, surrounded by pastel-colored palazzi, makes a colorful spectacle for visitors.

Piazza Campo de' Fiori • Market open 8 a.m. to 2 p.m., closed Sun. • Bus: 40, 46, 62, 64, 70, 81, 116, 492, 628 • Tram: 8

GOOD **EATS**

■ **GUSTO WINE BAR**
Drop into this wine bar and restaurant near Ara Pacis for a refreshing *aperitivo.*
Via della Frezza 23, 06 3226 273

■ **MAGNOLIA BAR**
This popular haunt sells both American- and Italian-style breakfasts. **Piazza Campo de' Fiori 4, 06 6830 9367,** €

■ **TAVERNA TRILUSSA**
This family-run trattoria in Trastevere serves classic Roman dishes. **Via del Politeama 23, 06 581 8918,** €€

Via del Governo Vecchio

2 Pop into **Cinzia** (*No. 45*) for second-hand apparel, **Cecilia e Omero** (*No. 68*) for 1970s styles, and **Tempi Moderni** (*No. 108*) or **Indecoroso** (*No. 67*) for outrageous bijoux and accessories.

Via del Governo Vecchio • Bus: 62, 64, 492

Chiostro del Bramante

3 Donato Bramante's Renaissance cloister, with its slender columns and arcades, invites visitors to linger. Don't miss Raphael's fresco, "The Sibyls," in the upper loggia, while the former monks' quarters host art and design exhibitions.

Arco della Pace 5 • 06 6880 9035 • Bus: 62, 64, 492

Piazza Navona

4 This splendid square represents the ultimate in baroque style. In December, don't miss out on the Christmas market held here.

Piazza Navona • Bus: 70, 81, 116, 186, 492

Pantheon

5 This is the one site that truly impressed Michelangelo upon his arrival in Rome. Eternally grand and tranquil, the rotunda seems to have the same temperature year-round, a boon on a hot day.

Piazza della Rotonda • 06 6830 0230 • Closed Jan. 1, May 1, and Dec. 25 • Bus: C3, 40, 46, 62, 63, 64, 70, 81, 87, 116, 119, 492, 628 • Tram: 8

Via di Campo Marzio

6 Once a training ground for Roman soldiers, the Field of Mars today features great boutiques, from **Davide Cenci** *(No. 1)* for men's fashion, to **Campo Marzio Design** *(No. 41)* for fine stationery.

Via di Campo Marzio • Bus: 52, 53, 61, 71, 80, 85, 116, 160

Luxury Shopping

7 The small triangular Piazza di San Lorenzo in Lucina hosts stores of **Bottega Veneta** *(No. 9)* and **La Martina** *(No. 18)*. Browse Via dei Condotti for more luxury brands, including **Battistoni** *(No. 60–61A)* for suits, shirts, and accessories for men and women.

Via dei Condotti • Metro: Spagna • Bus: 116, 117, 119

A Stroll to the Pincio

8 From Trinità dei Monti, skirt the Villa Borghese gardens to arrive at the Pincio. Here, enjoy the shade of the pine trees and the panoramic terrace dotted with busts and statues.

W side of the Villa Borghese • Metro: Flaminio, Line A

Ara Pacis

9 The Altar of Peace, one of Rome's greatest ancient monuments, is carved with realistic portraits of the Emperor Augustus's family.

Lungotevere in Augusta • en.arapacis.it • 06 06 08 • €€€ • Closed Mon. • Metro: Spagna, Flaminio, Line A

Trastevere

10 After dinner (see p. 158), head to **Big Mama** (see p. 158) or **Ombre Rosse** *(Piazza San Egidio 12)* for drinks and live music.

Between Lungotevere R. Sanzio, Via Garibaldi, and Viale di Trastevere • Bus: 280

Trinità dei Monti on the Spanish Steps is the starting point for a beautiful walk to the Pincio.

WHIRLWIND TOURS

Rome in a Weekend with Kids

Designed around the theme of ancient Rome, this route keeps to the southern part of the historic center.

6 Piazza Navona (see pp. 31, 123) Rome's most festive square is filled with fountains, sidewalk cafés, and the city's best street performers—a great place to relax at the end of any day.

PIAZZA CAVOUR

BORGO

Castel Sant'Angelo

PONTE CAVOUR

VIA DELLA CONCILIAZIONE

PONTE VITTORIO EMANUELE II

PONTE SANT' ANGELO

PONTE UMBERTO

VIA D. SCROFA

CORSO VITT. EMANUELE II

San Luigi dei Francesi

Sant' Agnese in Agone

6 Piazza Navona

Panthe

LARGO D TORRE ARGENTIN

VIA GIULIA

PONTE G. MAZZINI

PIAZZA FARNESE

PIAZZA CAMPO DE' FIORI

Villa Farnesina

Palazzo Farnese

Palazzo Corsini

PONTE SISTO

VIA ARENULA

GHETTO

G i a n i c o l o

Santa Maria in Trastevere

Tevere

LUNG. SANZIO

PONTE GARIBALDI

Isola Tiberina

Santa Cecilia in Trastevere

1 Bocca della Verità (see pp. 30, 166) The ominous Mouth of Truth has been spooking youngsters (and their parents) since medieval times. From the front of the church, turn left onto Via della Greca and walk one block.

**ROME WITH KIDS DAY 1   DISTANCE: 7 MILES (11.3 KM)
TIME: 6 HOURS   METRO START: CIRCO MASSIMO, LINE B**

WHIRLWIND TOURS

⑤ Time Elevator (see p. 31)
Travel back in time to the founding of Rome in this multimedia extravaganza. Turn left out of the Time Elevator, and follow a series of short streets west for about ten minutes to Corso del Rinascimento and Piazza Navona.

Map labels:

VIA DEL CORSO

VIA DUE MACELLI

VIA DEL TRITONE

PIAZZA BARBERINI

Palazzo Barberini

Fontana di Trevi

Quirinale

Time Elevator

Palazzo del Quirinale

San Carlo alle Quattro Fontane

Sant'Andrea al Quirinale

VIA DEL QUIRINALE

PIAZZA DELLA REPUBBLICA

Repubblica Ⓜ

Museo Nazionale Romano

⑤

Pal. Doria Pamphili

Palazzo Colonna

VIA NAZIONALE

Viminale

PIAZZA DELL' ESQUILINO

Santa Maria Maggiore

PIAZZA VENEZIA

Il Gesù

Mon. a Vitt. Emanuele II

Santa Maria in Aracoeli

VIA DEI FORI IMPERIALI

Capitolino

San Pietro in Vincoli

VIA CAVOUR

Ⓜ Cavour

VIA G. LANZA

VIA MERULANA

Musei Capitolini

Foro Romano

PARCO DI TRAIANO

Esquilino

Teatro di Marcello

Arco di Costantino

Ⓜ Colosseo

PIAZZA DEL COLOSSEO

④ Colosseo

Domus Aurea

VIA LABICANA

San Clemente

MONTE PALATINO

Palatino

VIA DEI CERCHI

San Gregorio Magno

VIA DI SAN GIOVANNI IN LATERANO

VIA CLAUDIA

①

Bocca la Verità

②

Circo Massimo

Ⓜ Circo Massimo

VILLA CELIMONTANA

③

Aventino

To Parco dell' Appia Antica

0 ——————— 1 kilometer
0 ——————— ½ mile

② Circo Massimo (see pp. 30, 166–167)
Now a field, the Circus Maximus was once the site of chariot races. At its eastern end, cross the Viale Aventino and take a taxi to the Via Appia Antica. Ask to be dropped at the Catacombe di San Callisto. The 118 bus also goes there but is very infrequent.

④ Colosseo (see pp. 31, 66–67)
Explore the ancient world's most celebrated stadium. From its western end, walk down the Via dei Fori Imperiali. Cross the Piazza Venezia onto Via del Corso, and turn right on Via dei Santi Apostoli.

③ Parco dell' Appia Antica (Catacombs) (see pp. 30–31) This park includes an ancient road and several underground cemeteries. Take a taxi back to Piazza di Porta Capena. Turn right on Via di San Gregorio, and walk north toward the Arco di Costantino (see p. 60).

Bocca della Verità

1 An urban myth tells that medieval priests used to put scorpions inside the Mouth of Truth to sting people—part of the legend that it bites liars. See if you and your kids can hold your nerve.

Santa Maria in Cosmedin, Piazza Bocca della Verità 18 • www.060608.it • 06 678 7759 • Donation • Metro: Circo Massimo, Line B • Bus: 44, 81, 95, 271, 628

Circo Massimo

2 Up to 250,000 people supported their favorite charioteers at a stadium that once stood in this park. Let your children run around and imagine the sound and fury of every race.

Via dei Cerchi and Via del Circo Massimo • www.060608.it • Metro: Circo Massimo, Line B • Bus: 81, 160, 175, 628 • Tram: 3

Parco dell' Appia Antica (Catacombs)

3 The **Via Appia,** one of the first Roman roads, and its surroundings now compose one of the city's largest parks. There are also creepy subterranean cemeteries here, including the

The pristine Parco dell' Appia Antica combines archaeological monuments and nature trails.

Catacombe di San Callisto (*Via Appia Antica 110–126, 06 513 0151, €€, closed Wed., Jan. 1, Feb, Easter Sun., and Dec. 25*), which contain the remains of early Christians, including many popes.

Via Appia Antica • www.parcoappiaantica.it • 06 512 6314

Colosseo

4 Almost 2,000 years ago, gladiators and wild beasts locked in deadly combat in front of thousands of spectators at this superbly preserved Roman stadium. The **gladiator dungeons** and the overview from the **third-tier terrace**—which must be booked in advance—will thrill your kids.

Piazza del Colosseo • www.060608i.it • 06 3996 7700 • €€€ • Closed Jan. 1 and Dec. 25 • Metro: Colosseo, Line B • Bus: C3, 60, 75, 81, 85, 87, 175 • Tram: 3

GOOD **EATS**

■ **HOSTARIA ANTICA ROMA**
Try Roman and Mediterranean specialties in an ancient building near the catacombs. **Via Appia Antica 87, 06 513 2888, €€€€**

■ **NAUMACHIA**
A kid-friendly pizzeria near the Colosseo serves up classic pizzas with popular toppings, as well as tasty pasta. **Via Celimontana 7, 06 700 2764, €€€**

Time Elevator

5 Roman history goes high tech at this multimedia experience in the heart of the old city. Go on a 45-minute journey through 2,700 years of local history by means of three panoramic screens, moving chairs, and surround sound. The same theater is used for two other shows: **"An Ode To Life,"** which chronicles Earth's history from the Big Bang to modern times, and **"Escape from Bane Manor,"** a scary house-of-horrors experience.

Via dei Santi Apostoli 20 • www.timeelevator.it • 06 6992 1823 • €€€ • Bus: 62, 63, 81, 85, 95, 117, 119, 160, 175, 492, 628, 630

Piazza Navona

6 Round out the day and rest your feet at Piazza Navona, where you'll find an abundance of cafés, elaborate fountains, and energetic street performers. It's a great place for kids and parents to indulge in a famous Roman gelato (ice cream) at the day's end.

Piazza Navona • Bus: 70, 81, 116, 186, 492

WHIRLWIND TOURS

Rome in a Weekend with Kids

Take in a broad sweep of history and a taste of the outdoors, with an ossuary, a zoo, a science museum, and the famous Spanish Steps.

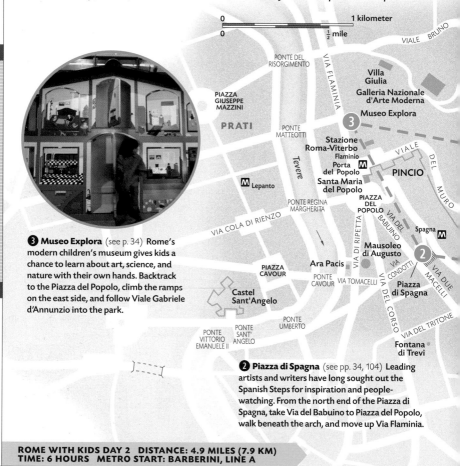

3 Museo Explora (see p. 34) Rome's modern children's museum gives kids a chance to learn about art, science, and nature with their own hands. Backtrack to the Piazza del Popolo, climb the ramps on the east side, and follow Viale Gabriele d'Annunzio into the park.

2 Piazza di Spagna (see pp. 34, 104) Leading artists and writers have long sought out the Spanish Steps for inspiration and people-watching. From the north end of the Piazza di Spagna, take Via del Babuino to Piazza del Popolo, walk beneath the arch, and move up Via Flaminia.

ROME WITH KIDS DAY 2   DISTANCE: 4.9 MILES (7.9 KM)
TIME: 6 HOURS   METRO START: BARBERINI, LINE A

❹ Villa Borghese (see pp. 35, 107) **Once the realm of wealthy Romans, this expansive park is a great place to bike, hike, and picnic. On the north side of the park, follow Viale del Giardino Zoologico to the zoo entrance.**

❺ Bioparco (see p. 35) **One of the world's oldest zoos now has natural habitats. Turn left out of the zoo, and follow Viale del Giardino Zoologico to Viale G. Rossini. Hop onto the 3 tram (toward Trastevere) or 19 (toward Gerani) and get off at Via Nomentana. Walk northeast.**

❻ Technotown (see p. 35) **Lodged in a mock-medieval castle, this museum unveils the mysteries of science and technology through interactive exhibits.**

❶ Santa Maria della Concezione dei Cappuccini (see pp. 34, 92–93) **The curiously arranged bones of Capuchin friars in the crypt are the main draw at this lovely baroque church. Walk two blocks down Via dei Cappuccini, and hang a right on Via Sistina to the top of the Spanish Steps.**

Santa Maria della Concezione dei Cappuccini

1 This 17th-century baroque church is renowned for its bone crypt, where the bones of around 4,000 Capuchin friars are preserved in startling ways. While some skeletons remain intact, most of the bones are used in elaborate—and often macabre—artworks or architectural details that decorate the five underground chapels. The names alone are enough to give you a chill: the **Crypt of the Skulls, Crypt of the Pelvises, Crypt of the Leg and Thigh Bones,** and **Crypt of the Three Skeletons.**

Via Vittorio Veneto 27 • www.cappucciniviaveneto.it • 06 487 1185 • Donation: minimum € • Closed Thurs. and noon–3 p.m. daily • Metro: Barberini, Line A • Bus: 52, 53, 63, 80, 95, 116

GOOD **EATS**

■ **CANTINA CANTARINI**
Humble yet high-quality cooking awaits a 15-minute walk from Via Veneto. Be prepared for tight seating. **Piazza Sallustio 12, 06 474 3341, €€€**

■ **PALATIUM**
This restaurant and wine bar near the Spanish Steps serves local cuisine from the Lazio region, with healthy, vegetable-rich dishes. **Via Frattina 94, 06 6920 2132, €€€**

Piazza di Spagna

2 Let your kids run off their energy going up and down the famed Spanish Steps. Some may not cherish the area's literary history, but they will certainly seek out the **Roman obelisk,** at the top of the steps, and **La Barcaccia**—the "leaking boat" fountain inspired by an actual boat that washed up in a flood—at the bottom.

Between Via dei Condotti and Via della Croce • Metro: Spagna, Line A

Museo Explora

3 Housed in an old bus pavilion, Rome's children's museum is an interactive place for kids to explore art, science, and nature in a hands-on environment where "touching, testing, and playing" are encouraged. Built like a small town, the museum divides activities into three age groups from infants through age 12. Explora operates on a "time-ticketing" system, with four entry times daily and a maximum of 1 hour and 45 minutes for each visit.

Via Flaminia 82 • www.mdbr.it • 06 361 3776 • €€ • Closed Mon., Jan. 1, and Dec. 25 • Metro: Flaminio, Line A

Villa Borghese

(4) Rome's version of Central Park offers amazing vistas over the Eternal City. There are many leafy avenues and wide-open spaces to run around and neoclassical temples to explore, as well as plenty of recreational distractions. Kids will love the **San Carlino puppet theater** (*Viale dei Bambini, 06 6992 2117*), which puts on weekend plays throughout the year. Villa Borghese also offers bike, skate, and Risciò (a kind of two- or four-person bike) rental, as well as rowboats in the **Giardino del Lago,** a lake graced by a famous water clock from 1867.

Between Via Flaminia and Via Pinciana • Metro: Flaminio, Spagna, Line A

Bioparco

(5) Founded in 1911, the Bioparco is one of Europe's oldest zoos. In recent years, modern enclosures have replaced cages including **Bear Valley, Wolves Woods,** the **Chimpanzee Village,** and an **African Savannah** exhibit. The zoo also boasts a large and diverse **Reptile House,** as well as habitats for lemurs and marmosets, African wild dogs, and pigmy hippos.

Viale del Giardino Zoologico 1 • www.bioparco.it • 06 360 8211 • €€€ • Bus: 217, 910 • Tram: 3, 19

Technotown

(6) Designed for kids from the ages of 8 to 17, Technotown is a cutting-edge science and technology museum that gives children hands-on experience with 3-D imagery, movie special effects, sound and music engineering, robots, lasers, and materials of the future. The museum resides on the grounds of the 19th-century noble mansion, Villa Torlonia.

Via Lazzaro Spallanzani 2 • 06 06 08 • €€ • Closed Mon. • Bus: 36, 60 Express, 62, 84, 90 Express, 140

New acquaintances are made at Rome's laid-back Bioparco.

PART 2

Rome's Neighborhoods

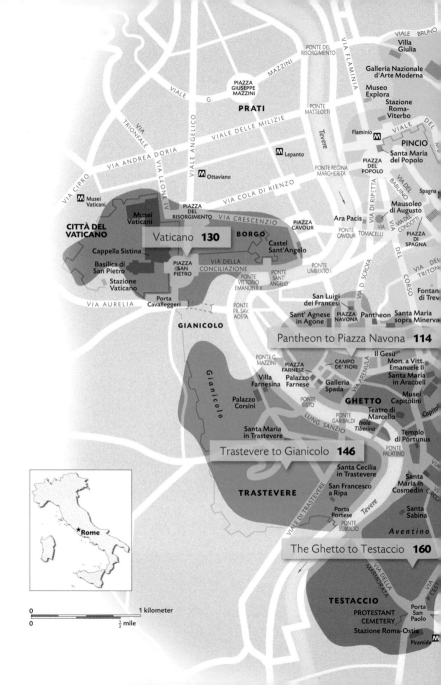

VIALE BRUNO

Villa Giulia

VIALE

G.

MAZZINI

PONTE DEL RISORGIMENTO

VIA FLAMINIA

Galleria Nazionale d'Arte Moderna

Museo Explora

PIAZZA GIUSEPPE MAZZINI

Stazione Roma-Viterbo

PRATI

VIALE ANGELICO

VIALE DELLE MILIZIE

PONTE MATTEOTTI

Tevere

Flaminio M

PINCIO

Santa Maria del Popolo

VIA TRIONFALE

VIA ANDREA DORIA

VIA LEONE IV

M Lepanto

PONTE REGINA MARGHERITA

PIAZZA DEL POPOLO

VIA DEL BABUINO

VIA CIPRO

M Ottaviano

VIA COLA DI RIENZO

VIA DI RIPETTA

Ara Pacis

Mausoleo di Augusto

Spagna

VIA DEI CONDOTTI

Musei Vaticani

PIAZZA DEL RISORGIMENTO

VIA CRESCENZIO

PIAZZA CAVOUR

PONTE CAVOUR

VIA TOMACELLI

PIAZZA DI SPAGNA

CITTÀ DEL VATICANO

Musei Vaticani

BORGO

Castel Sant'Angelo

VIA DEL CORSO

VIA DEL TRITON

Vaticano 130

Cappella Sistina

Basilica di San Pietro

PIAZZA SAN PIETRO

VIA DELLA CONCILIAZIONE

PONTE VITTORIO EMANUELE II

PONTE SANT' ANGELO

PONTE UMBERTO I

VIA D. SCROFA

Fontan di Trev

Stazione Vaticano

Porta Cavalleggeri

PONTE PR. SAV. AOSTA

San Luigi dei Francesi

VIA AURELIA

GIANICOLO

Sant' Agnese in Agone

PIAZZA NAVONA

Pantheon

Santa Maria sopra Minerva

Pantheon to Piazza Navona **114**

PONTE G. MAZZINI

PIAZZA FARNESE

CAMPO DE' FIORI

VIA ARENULA

Il Gesù

Mon. a Vitt. Emanuele II

Villa Farnesina

Palazzo Farnese

Santa Maria in Aracoeli

G
i
a
n
i
c
o
l
o

Galleria Spada

Musei Capitolini

Palazzo Corsini

PONTE SISTO

GHETTO

Capitol

PONTE GARIBALDI

Teatro di Marcello

Santa Maria in Trastevere

LUNG. SANZIO

PONTE PALATINO

Isola Tiberina

Templo di Portunus

Trastevere to Gianicolo **146**

Santa Cecilia in Trastevere

Santa Maria in Cosmedin

TRASTEVERE

San Francesco a Ripa

Tevere

VIA CIRCO

Santa Sabina

VIALE DI TRASTEVERE

Porta Portese

PONTE SUBLICIO

Aventino

The Ghetto to Testaccio **160**

★Rome

VIA DELLA MARMORATA

VIA P. CEST

TESTACCIO

PROTESTANT CEMETERY

Porta San Paolo

0   1 kilometer

0   ½ mile

Stazione Roma-Ostia

Piramide M

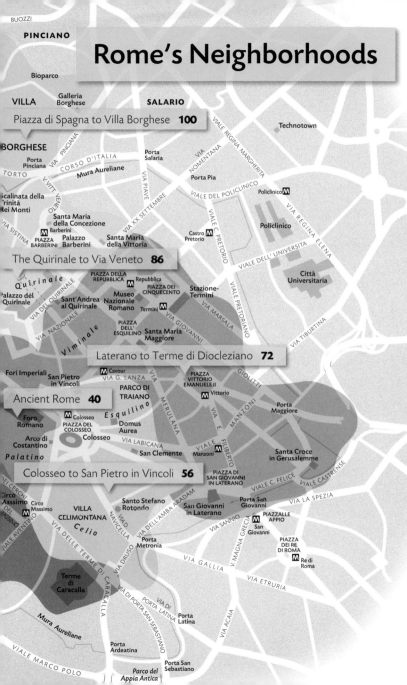

Rome's Neighborhoods

BUOZZI

PINCIANO

Bioparco

VILLA   Galleria
         Borghese   SALARIO

Piazza di Spagna to Villa Borghese **100**

BORGHESE   Technotown

Porta   Porta
Pinciana   Salaria
         CORSO D'ITALIA
TORTO   Mura Aureliane
                         Porta Pia

scalinata della   VIALE DEL POLICLINICO   Policlinico M
Trinità   VIA REGINA MARGHERITA
dei Monti
                         Castro   Policlinico
Santa Maria   Pretorio
della Concezione
Barberini   VIALE DELL' UNIVERSITA
PIAZZA   Palazzo   Santa Maria   Città
BARBERINI Barberini della Vittoria   Universitaria

The Quirinale to Via Veneto **86**

Quirinale
                 PIAZZA DELLA
                 REPUBBLICA   M Repubblica
Palazzo dèl   Sant'Andrea PIAZZA DEI
Quirinale   al Quirinale CINQUECENTO Stazione-
              Museo   Termini
              Nazionale
              Romano   Termini
                 PIAZZA
                 DELL'
Viminale   ESQUILINO Santa Maria
                            Maggiore

Laterano to Terme di Diocleziano **72**

Fori Imperiali M Cavour   PIAZZA
San Pietro   VIA G. LANZA   VITTORIO
in Vincoli   EMANUELE.II
              PARCO DI   M Vittorio
              TRAIANO   Porta
Ancient Rome **40**   Maggiore

Foro   M Colosseo   Esquilino
Romano   PIAZZA DEL
Arco di   COLOSSEO   Domus
Costantino Colosseo   Aurea   Santa Croce
Palatino   VIA LABICANA   in Gerusalemme
                   San Clemente   Manzoni

Colosseo to San Pietro in Vincoli **56**

                            PIAZZA DI
                            SAN GIOVANNI
                            IN LATERANO
Circo   Santo Stefano   San Giovanni   Porta San
Massimo Circo   Rotondo   in Laterano   Giovanni   PIAZZALE
         Massimo   APPIO
         VILLA   San Giovanni   M San
         CELIMONTANA   Celio   Giovanni   PIAZZA
                            Porta   DEI RE
                            Metronia   DI ROMA
                                                          M Re di
                                                            Roma
Terme
di
Caracalla

Mura Aureliane

VIALE MARCO POLO

Porta
Ardeatina
                Porta San
                Sebastiano
         Parco del
         Appia Antica

Ancient Rome

According to legend, Rome's first king, Romulus, founded the city on the Palatino (Palatine Hill) in 753 B.C. Later nobles and emperors built grand villas there. In the valley below, the Foro Romano (Roman Forum) acted as the city center, housing the most important political, financial, and civic buildings. At its northwestern end rises the Capitolino (Capitoline Hill). Now home to the Piazza del Campidoglio and Musei Capitolini (Capitoline Museums), it was once the religious center of Rome, where the greatest temples rose and where triumphal and devotional processions ended. As the city and the empire expanded, the Foro Romano did not have enough space for the city's civic buildings, so the Fori Imperiali (Imperial Forums) were built over time. These five public squares northeast of the Foro Romano owe their existence to the dictator Julius Caesar and later imperial leaders Augustus, Vespasian, Nerva, and Trajan, each seeking to leave his stamp on Rome.

❶ **A statue of a vestal priestess stands in the Casa delle Vestali in the Foro Romano.**

Ancient Rome

Ancient Rome's most extensive ruins cluster tightly together in the heart of the modern city.

⑤ Santa Maria in Aracoeli (see pp. 46–47) This Franciscan church dominated the Capitolino before the neighboring Vittorio Emanuele II Monument, the Vittoriano, was built. Exit from the right aisle, and follow the winding Via di San Pietro in Carcere to the bottom of the hill.

⑥ Fori Imperiali (see pp. 47–48) The Via dei Fori Imperiali, a modern road, partially obscures five public squares built between the first century B.C. and the second century A.D. Take the staircase near Colonna di Traiano to reach the entrance to the Mercati.

⑦ Mercati di Traiano (see p. 49) Emperor Trajan built the so-called Markets beside the Foro di Traiano. The complex was actually used for administrative functions and today houses the Museo dei Fori Imperiali.

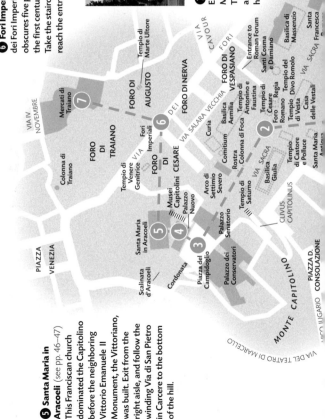

PIAZZA VENEZIA

VIA IV NOVEMBRE

Colonna di Traiano

Mercati di Traiano ⑦

FORO DI TRAIANO

Tempio di Venere Genitrice

VIA

Fori Imperiali

FORO DI CESARE

FORO DI ⑥ AUGUSTO

DEI

Tempio di Marte Ultore

VIA CAVOUR

FORO DI NERVA

VIA SALARA VECCHIA

Santa Maria in Aracoeli ⑤

Musei Capitolini ④ Palazzo Nuovo

Arco di Settimio Severo

Curia

Rostra Colonna di Foca

Comitium

Tempio di Antonino e Faustina

Basilica Aemilia

Entrance to Roman Forum

FORO DI VESPASIANO

Santi Cosma e Damiano

Tempio di Foca

Tempio di Cesare

Foro Regia Romano

Tempio del Divo Romolo

Basilica di Massenzio

Scalinata d'Aracoeli

Palazzo Senatore

Tempio di Saturno

Tempio di Castore e Polluce

VIA SACRA

Tempio di Vesta

Casa delle Vestali

VIA SACRA Santa Francesca

Cordonata

Palazzo dei Conservatori

Piazza del Campidoglio ③

CLIVUS CAPITOLINUS

Basilica Giulia

VIA SACRA

Santa Maria Antiqua

② Tempio Divo Romolo

IMPERIALI

Antiquarium Forense

Colosseo Ⓜ

MONTE CAPITOLINO

ARCO DI GIARIO

PIAZZA D. CONSOLAZIONE

VIA DEL TEATRO DI MARCELLO

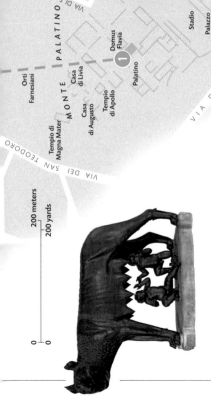

④ Musei Capitolini (see p. 46) Set in two buildings designed by Michelangelo, the Capitoline Museums house one of the world's best sculpture collections. Enter through the Palazzo dei Conservatori on the square's south side. Take the staircase to the right of the Palazzo Nuovo.

③ Piazza del Campidoglio (see p. 45) Michelangelo designed this elegant square and its surrounding buildings in the 16th century. The piazza turns its back on the ancient city with its forums built by emperors and opens toward the "new Rome" of the Renaissance.

② Foro Romano (see pp. 50–51) Follow the Via Sacra through Rome's ancient heart, from the Arco di Tito to the Arco di Settimio Severo, detouring for the Basilica di Massenzio and Casa delle Vestali. Leave from the northwestern end and climb the Capitolino.

① Palatino (see p. 44) Start at the Palatino and explore the monumental Domus Flavia, a first-century A.D. imperial palace. Peer over the Foro Romano from the Orti Farnesiani, then descend into the ruins at the Arco di Tito.

0 | 200 meters
0 | 200 yards

VIA DEI SAN TEODORO

Tempio di
Magna Mater

Orti
Farnesiani

MONTE PALATINO

Casa
di Augusto

Casa
di Livia

Tempio
di Apollo

Domus
Flavia

1 Palatino

Stadio

Palazzo
Settimio
Severo

VIA DEI CERCHI

VIA DI S. BONAVENTURA

Arco
di Tito

Tempio di
Venere e Roma

VIA SACRA

PIAZZA
DEL
COLOSSEO

**ANCIENT ROME   DISTANCE: 1.5 MILES (2.4 KM)
TIME: APPROX. 6 HOURS   METRO: COLOSSEO, LINE B**

ANCIENT ROME

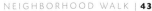

Palatino

1 Iron Age excavations, republican villas, the remains of temples, and imperial palaces pepper the Palatino, or Palatine Hill. A visit to this poorly labeled archaeological site requires a bit of patience and decoding. Begin in the first-century **Domus Flavia**, a sprawling villa built over two levels by the emperors of the Flavian dynasty, complete with central heating, extensive fountains, and massive banquet halls. The building was part of an architectural revolution in which Emperor Domitian and architect Rabirius collaborated to create a palace that would awe visitors with its height, scale, and innovation. Using brick-and-concrete masonry, they crafted a semicircular dining hall with a hemispherical roof, a walking track suitable for summer strolls, and a dining hall with 100-foot (30 m) ceilings. The surfaces were covered in marble veneers quarried all over the empire.

The **Antiquarium del Palatino** (Palatine Museum) displays finds from the palace and other digs on the hill. Nearby on the hill's southwestern slopes, the **Casa di Augusto** (House of Augustus), the first emperor's villa, preserves elegant frescoes depicting architecture and fanciful scenes. The **Orti Farnesiani,** planted over palace ruins, recall the botanical gardens of the noble Farnese family that once occupied the area. The **Domus Tiberiana,** an imperial villa built by Tiberius, was refashioned by Nero after the fire of A.D. 64.

Via San Gregorio 30 • www.060608.it • €€€ • Closed Jan. 1, May 1, and Dec. 25 (Casa di Augusto closed Tues. and Fri.) • Metro: Colosseo, Line B

SAVVY **TRAVELER**

The best vantage for appreciating the Foro Romano is from the viewing platform on the Palatino. This spot, once the foundations of Emperor Tiberius's palace, provides a bird's-eye view over the footprint of the Casa delle Vestali and the ancient urban center.

Foro Romano

2 See pp. 50–51.

Via Salara Vecchia 5/6 • www.060608.it • €€€ • Closed Jan. 1, May 1, and Dec. 25 • Metro: Colosseo, Line B

Renaissance palaces, two of which comprise the Musei Capitolini, line the Piazza del Campidoglio.

Piazza del Campidoglio

3 The Piazza del Campidoglio can be approached via a staircase from the Foro Romano. Pope Paul III Farnese commissioned Michelangelo to design the square in 1536. The trapezoidal piazza with its three buildings lies in the depression between the Capitolino's two peaks. Facing each other across the square, the **Palazzo dei Conservatori** and the **Palazzo Nuovo** together form the Musei Capitolini (see p. 46), and the **Palazzo Senatorio,** the modern-day mayor's office. The facade of the Palazzo Senatorio, decorated with statues of river gods, shows the Nile deities on the left and the Tiber's on the right, as well as a granite statue restored to resemble Roma, the goddess that protected the city. A 1996 copy of a second-century A.D. Roman bronze **statue of Emperor Marcus Aurelius** adorns the center of the piazza. The original is inside the Musei Capitolini.

Piazza del Campidoglio • Metro: Colosseo, Line B

Musei Capitolini

4 The original collection was established by Pope Sixtus IV in 1471, even before Michelangelo built the present structures, making the Musei Capitolini (Capitoline Museums) the oldest public museums in the West. Over the course of subsequent centuries, various popes donated fine ancient sculptures of marble and bronze to the museums. On the ground floor of the Palazzo dei Conservatori, the remains of a colossal **statue of Constantine,** including his head, knee, hand, and biceps, sit in separate pieces against a wall in the entrance courtyard. Upstairs, seek out a symbol of the city: the **Lupa Capitolina,** a medieval bronze wolf long mistaken for an ancient work. The **Esedra di Marco Aurelio** houses the original of the equestrian statue of the emperor whose copy stands in the square outside, as well as the fragments of a colossal bronze statue of Emperor Constantine. Nearby, remains of the **Temple of Jupiter Optimus Maximus** have been unearthed. The second floor of the Palazzo dei Conservatori exhibits oil paintings, including Caravaggio's famous **"Fortune Teller."** The neighboring **Palazzo Nuovo,** reached through a subterranean tunnel, displays ancient sculpture. Look for the **Dying Gaul**—this celebrated marble statue shows a wounded warrior in the last moments of his life. In its own room off the main hall, the **Capitoline Venus** covers herself when caught in the act of bathing.

Piazza del Campidoglio 1 • www.museicapitolini.org • €€€ • Closed Mon., Dec. 24, and Dec. 31 • Metro: Colosseo, Line B

Santa Maria in Aracoeli

5 Built in the sixth century on the ruins of a temple dedicated to the goddess Juno, the church of Santa Maria in Aracoeli (St. Mary of the Altar of Heaven) ranks as one of Rome's most ancient Christian sites. According to legend, it was founded near the location in which a pagan sibyl foretold the coming of a messiah. The structure's dour brick exterior gives way to a highly embellished interior space that takes the form of a hall whose aisles are separated

ANCIENT ROME

by granite and marble columns plundered from ancient buildings. The floor is an intricate **12th-century mosaic,** also made from repurposed ancient materials. In the Bufalini Chapel in the right aisle near the main entrance, **Pinturicchio's frescoes** from the mid-1480s cover three walls and the ceiling, depicting scenes from the life of the Franciscan friar San Bernardino of Siena.

Piazza del Campidoglio, Scala dell'Arche Capitolina 14 • 06 6976 3839 • Closed 12:30–3p.m. • Metro: Colosseo, Line B

Fori Imperiali

6 Not one forum but five cluster together here. They include the Foro di Traiano, Foro di Augusto, Foro di Cesare, Foro di Pace (Forum of Peace), and Foro di Nerva, all named after the emperors who built them, except for the Foro di Pace built by Vespasian. Unfortunately, you can't walk through them, but you can admire

A sweep of the Fori Imperiali shows the Foro di Traiano on the left, dating from A.D. 113.

them from the roadway that overlooks them. By the late republic, the Foro Romano (see pp. 50–51) was bursting with buildings, monuments, arches, and altars. When Julius Caesar rose to power, he followed the republican custom of building and renovating structures on the Foro Romano, but he also began a new tradition by building his own forum.

The **Foro di Cesare** was a planned public space consisting of a temple dedicated to Venus fronted by a paved square and flanked by porticoes with shops and workshops for commercial use. External walls separated it from the adjacent Foro Romano. Caesar's successor Augustus, the first emperor, followed suit, building a forum with a temple to Mars. Three columns and its podium stand out among the rubble in the **Foro di Augusto.** Trajan built the most impressive forum, the **Foro di Traiano,** which features the 125-foot-tall (38 m) **Colonna di Traiano** (Trajan's Column), inaugurated in A.D. 113. A series of carved scenes with 2,600 figures spiral up the marble column, recounting the emperor's military successes in Dacia (Romania) and highlighting the engineering innovations that made them possible.

After the fall of the empire in the fifth century, the Fori Imperiali fell into a state of abandonment. Structures were looted and dismantled, and the area became a marginal suburb of the city. The rediscovery of the Fori began under Napoleon and intensified over a century later under Mussolini. The Fascist dictator both obscured and uncovered parts of the Fori Imperiali, building his Via dell'Impero—today's Via dei Fori Imperiali—while initiating digs on either side of this infamous parade route.

Via dei Fori Imperiali • www.060608.it • Metro: Colosseo, Line B

GOOD **EATS**

■ LA CARBONARA
This trattoria not far from the Fori Imperiali provides brisk and brusque service and hearty, cheap Roman cuisine—a major draw for locals and visitors.
**Via Panisperna 214,
06 482 5176, €€**

■ ENOTECA PROVINCIA ROMANA
This wine bar near the Mercati di Traiano serves local wine and food made with ingredients sourced exclusively from Rome and Rome's suburbs.
**Via del Foro Traiano 82/84,
06 6766 2424, €**

■ MIA MARKET
Also in the ancient center, salads, sandwiches, and soups are made with the highest quality ingredients.
**Via Panisperna 225,
06 4782 4611, €**

ANCIENT ROME

Walking in the footsteps of the ancients on Via Biberatica in the Mercati di Traiano

Mercati di Traiano

7 The Mercati di Traiano (Trajan's Markets), a vast administrative complex, cuts its way into the southern slopes of the Quirinale (Quirinal Hill). Indeed, its architect, Apollodorus of Damascus, who also designed the Foro di Traiano (see p. 48), excavated a large part of the Quirinale to accommodate the structure's exedra (semicircular recess). Set on three separate street levels, the site is a maze of more than a hundred offices and halls. Along the streets, taverns or shops selling food once occupied alcove-like indentations. A museum, the **Museo dei Fori Imperiali,** which traces the history of Rome's Fori Imperiali, forms part of the site. Each room covers one of the imperial forums. Trajan's Markets often have contemporary art exhibitions. Be sure to climb up to the **Giardino delle Milizie** for panoramic views.

Via IV Novembre 94 • www.mercatiditraiano.it • €€€ • Closed Mon., Jan. 1, and Dec. 25 • Metro: Colosseo, Line B

Foro Romano

These sprawling ruins attest to the rise of ancient Rome—and to its fall.

The Foro Romano sits in a valley beneath the Palatino.

During the thousand years it was in use, the Foro Romano (Roman Forum) evolved from a primitive marketplace into the command center of an empire. Home to Rome's most important legal, political, and triumphal monuments, the forum also served as an area for public gatherings and celebrations. Following the fall of the Roman Empire, centuries of neglect, plundering, and natural disasters have taken their toll, leaving most buildings in ruins and only five still reasonably intact.

■ Triumphal Arches

The **Via Sacra** (Sacred Route) ran the length of the forum. At the southeastern end, the **Arco di Tito** marks Emperor Titus's deification and victories in Judea. At its northwestern end stands the **Arco di Settimio Severo** of A.D. 203. The triple arch celebrates Emperor Septimius Severus's campaigns in the province of Parthia (Iran), one of Rome's last conquests.

■ Curia

Slightly southeast of the Arco di Settimio Severo, the Curia (Senate House), begun by Julius Caesar, was still under construction at his death in 44 B.C. The single enormous room once accommodated hundreds of senators whose benches rested on the **inlaid marble floor.** Its geometric pattern is made up of stones quarried in North Africa, Greece, and Asia Minor, all conquered territories.

■ Divine Rulers

When the senate deified emperors, they dedicated temples to them. Close to each other in the center of the forum, temples venerated Julius Caesar and a divine couple, Antonino (Antoninus in Latin) and Faustina.

IN **THE KNOW**

The first major digs on the Foro Romano began in 1800. Before the excavations, 30 feet (9 m) of debris and river silt covered most of what visitors see today. The mud and rubble buried half of the Arco di Settimio Severo and much of the Tempio di Antonino e Faustina.

■ Casa delle Vestali

The Casa delle Vestali (House of the Vestal Virgins) lies on the Via Sacra as it runs northwest down the Palatino. A group of priestesses lived in this sumptuous villa and maintained a sacred flame, which burned in a round temple to the goddess Vesta beside their home. Rooms surrounded the **atrium,** now a lawn. The Vestal Virgins lived here during 30 years of service that began in childhood.

■ Court of Law

Opposite the Casa delle Vestali, the **Basilica di Massenzio** was a court of law begun in the early fourth century A.D. by Emperor Maxentius and finished by Constantine. Its three aisles, made of poured concrete clad in brick, were once veneered in marble. Today just one aisle survives.

ANCIENT ROME

Via Salara Vecchia 5/6 • www.060608.it • €€€ • Closed Jan. 1, May 1, and Dec. 25 • Metro: Colosseo, Line B

Imperial City

By the first century B.C., Rome's sphere of influence reached around the Mediterranean and across western Europe, with the city itself as the glittering centerpiece. Political tensions in the senate led to power struggles and a civil war from which Julius Caesar emerged as dictator. His assassination in 44 B.C. sparked further conflicts. From 27 B.C., power rested with Caesar's chosen heir, Augustus, the first in a line of emperors who left their mark on the city.

The Colonna di Traiano towers over the ruins of the Fori Imperiali, with the baroque church of SS Nome di Maria in the background (above). Emperor Vespasian began the Colosseo in A.D. 72 (right).

Building for Glory

The emperors, good and bad, knew the value of lavish gestures and created impressive buildings and monuments to excite and intimidate their citizens, visitors, and prisoners of war. Drawing on a vast resource of talent, labor, and slaves, the emperors turned Rome into a grand city to match its status as the capital of the empire—attaching their names and prestige to temples, theaters, stadia, columns, and triumphal arches. They also built on a grand scale to ensure their place in history.

A Golden Age

By the end of the first century A.D., Rome had become the world's largest city, with a population of about one million. Its grand avenues and squares shone with marble, mosaics, and gilding and bristled with splendid sculpture and decorative flourishes. Obelisks, like the one that stands in the **Piazza del Popolo** (see p. 105), were carried back in triumph from Egypt. Sculptures were shipped in from Greece and emulated by Roman sculptors. Under a series of capable emperors, the empire reached its greatest extent, and Rome was enjoying its Golden Age.

Decline & Fall

Yet over time, the city acquired a reputation for complacency and corruption. In A.D. 293, under Emperor Diocletian, the imperial capital was moved from Rome to Milan. Later, Emperor Constantine (304–337) moved the capital east to Constantinople (now Istanbul).

By the early fifth century, the authority of the empire was collapsing in the face of revolt and invasions. In 475, the Western Empire formally ended as Odoacer the Goth took power in Italy. Rome fell into ruins, awaiting rediscovery almost a thousand years later, during the Renaissance.

SIX **EMPERORS**

Tiberius (reigned A.D. 14–37) Celebrated general became a recluse and moved to Capri.

Caligula (37–41) Reportedly became a cruel, vindictive, and deluded tyrant. Assassinated.

Nero (54–68) Empire builder, promoter of culture, but also a murderous tyrant.

Trajan (98–117) Brilliant general, just ruler. The empire was now at its greatest extent.

Hadrian (117–138) Good administrator and energetic builder, who traveled widely.

Marcus Aurelius (161–180) Philosopher-king and writer who battled Rome's enemies.

ANCIENT ROME

Day Trips

As captivating and rich as Rome's historical center may be, take time to visit its suburbs, where more ancient sites await. At Ostia Antica, town houses and apartment blocks have been well preserved, while Etruscan burial mounds and imperial and late Renaissance villas are less than an hour's journey from the city.

ANCIENT ROME

■ OSTIA ANTICA

This ancient port town, 13 miles (21 km) southwest of Rome's Stazione Lido, played an important commercial and administrative role during the empire. A planned Roman town, the city may have had as many as 100,000 residents. The streets were laid out on a grid with a forum at its center and a theater, apartment buildings, public baths, and temples along its main avenue. Be sure to look for the many **Mithraic sanctuaries,** underground cult spaces dedicated to the Persian god Mithras.

www.archeoroma.beniculturali.it. • Train: Ostia Antica, Roma–Lido line

■ CERVETERI NECROPOLIS

In the ancient Etruscan settlement of Cerveteri, in the countryside north of Rome, wealthy citizens built and decorated elaborate tombs. Some tombs are circular in shape, others square, and many are embellished with carvings and frescoes.

Bus: Cornelia Metro stop to Cerveteri. Then walk or local bus to site

■ VILLA D'ESTE

After narrowly losing the election for pope in 1550, Cardinal Ippolito d'Este retreated to Tivoli, 20 miles (32 km) east of Rome. In a grand gesture aimed at asserting his power, Cardinal d'Este, with the artist-architect Pirro Ligorio, transformed his humble monastery into a magnificent villa with fountains spilling from a terraced hillside. The villa underwent a long restoration to revive its innovative water features, which include a fountain equipped with water pipes that play music. The villa itself is painted with lively, fanciful frescoes from the late 16th century.

Piazza Trento 5, Tivoli • www.villadestetivoli .info • 0774 332 920 • €€ • Closed Mon. • Train: Stazione Tivoli, Line Roma–Pescara

Hundreds of fountains and water features adorn the Renaissance gardens of the Villa d'Este.

■ VILLA ADRIANA

In the plains below Tivoli, Emperor Hadrian built ancient Rome's largest and most lavish imperial villa in the second century A.D. Occupying twice the area of the city of Pompeii, its architecture was partly influenced by the emperor's foreign travels around his empire. The **Canopus,** a canal terminating at a grand banquet hall, evokes Egypt; the **Doric Hall** and **Temple of Venus** are nods to Greece, while the so-called **Maritime Theater,** living quarters surrounded by a moat, is pure Roman innovation.

Via di Villa Adriana, Tivoli • www.060608.it • 06 3996 7900 • €€ • Closed Jan. 1, Dec. 25 • Metro: Ponte Mammolo, Line B, Cotral bus to Villa Adriana

■ CASTELLI ROMANI

In antiquity and the Renaissance, noble families built country homes in the hills southeast of Rome. The area, known as the Castelli Romani, or Roman castles, is made up of 13 quiet villages. One of these, **Nemi,** perches above a lake that the ancients called Diana's Mirror after the Roman goddess of the moon and hunting. Visit Nemi for a stroll in its medieval quarter, swim in its lake, or see models of ancient ships in the **Museo delle Navi Romane** (*Via di Diana 13, 06 941 9665, €, Closed Jan. 1, May 1, and Dec. 25*).

Metro: Anagnina, Line A, then Cotral bus to Genzano Romano, then Cotral bus to Nemi

Colosseo to San Pietro in Vincoli

The first-century Flavian Amphitheater, more commonly known as the Colosseo (Colosseum), dominates the area east of the Foro Romano. The largest arena in the Roman world, the Colosseo was the city's main venue for public spectacle for 450 years. Later, Christian communities flourished at nearby churches, including Santi Giovanni e Paolo and Santo Stefano Rotondo. The church of San Pietro in Vincoli (St. Peter in Chains) is home to Michelangelo's statue of the Old Testament prophet Moses. Beside the Colosseo, the Arco di Costantino (Arch of Constantine) celebrates that emperor's victory at the Milvian Bridge in A.D. 312, during an internal power struggle. These two monuments occupy a valley bounded by the Esquilino and Oppio (Esquiline and Oppian Hills) in the north and the Celio (Caelian Hill) in the south and east.

◀ **Statues once occupied the second- and third-story arches of the Colosseo, which has been a focal point of Rome for 2,000 years.**

Colosseo to San Pietro in Vincoli

The Colosseo and surrounding hills provide a look at the daily life of ancient Romans and the changes that came about when the empire fell and the city was Christianized.

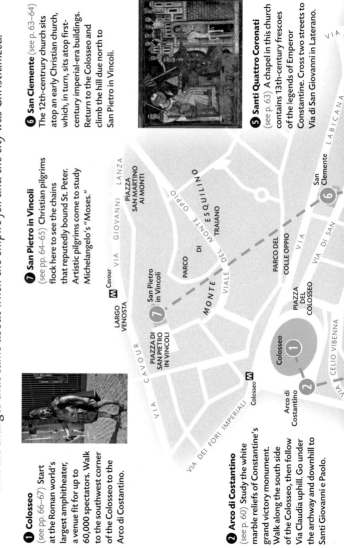

❶ Colosseo
(see pp. 66–67) **Start at the Roman world's largest amphitheater,** a venue fit for up to 60,000 spectators. Walk to the southwest corner of the Colosseo to the Arco di Costantino.

❷ Arco di Costantino
(see p. 60) **Study the white marble reliefs of Constantine's grand victory monument.** Walk along the south side of the Colosseo, then follow Via Claudia uphill. Go under the archway and downhill to Santi Giovanni e Paolo.

❼ San Pietro in Vincoli
(see pp. 64–65) **Christian pilgrims flock here to see the chains** that reputedly bound St. Peter. Artistic pilgrims come to study Michelangelo's "Moses."

❻ San Clemente (see p. 63–64)
The 12th-century church sits atop an early Christian church, which, in turn, sits atop first-century imperial-era buildings. Return to the Colosseo and climb the hill due north to San Pietro in Vincoli.

❺ Santi Quattro Coronati
(see p. 63) **A chapel in this church contains 13th-century frescoes** of the legends of Emperor Constantine. Cross two streets to Via di San Giovanni in Laterano.

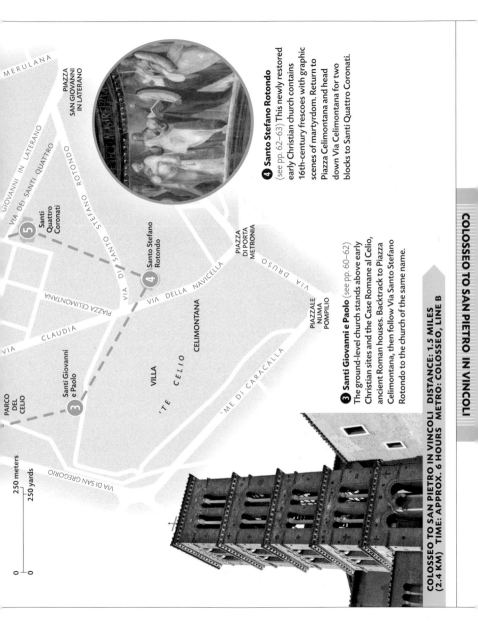

4 Santo Stefano Rotondo
(see pp. 62–63) This newly restored early Christian church contains 16th-century frescoes with graphic scenes of martyrdom. Return to Piazza Celimontana and head down Via Celimontana for two blocks to Santi Quattro Coronati.

3 Santi Giovanni e Paolo (see pp. 60–62) The ground-level church stands above early Christian sites and the Case Romane al Celio, ancient Roman houses. Backtrack to Piazza Celimontana, then follow Via Santo Stefano Rotondo to the church of the same name.

COLOSSEO TO SAN PIETRO IN VINCOLI DISTANCE: 1.5 MILES (2.4 KM) TIME: APPROX. 6 HOURS METRO: COLOSSEO, LINE B

Map labels:
MERULANA
PIAZZA SAN GIOVANNI IN LATERANO
GIOVANNI IN LATERANO
VIA DEI SANTI QUATTRO
5 Santi Quattro Coronati
VIA DI SANTO STEFANO ROTONDO
PIAZZA CELIMONTANA
4 Santo Stefano Rotondo
VIA DELLA NAVICELLA
PIAZZA DI PORTA METRONIA
VIA DRUSO
CELIMONTANA
PIAZZALE NUMA POMPILIO
CLAUDIA
VIA
VILLA 'TE CELIO
ME DI CARACALLA
3 Santi Giovanni e Paolo
PARCO DEL CELIO
VIA DI SAN GREGORIO
0 250 meters
0 250 yards

Colosseo

See pp. 66–67.

Piazza del Colosseo • www.060608.it • 06 3996 7700 • €€€ • Closed Jan. 1 and Dec. 25 • Metro: Colosseo, Line B • Bus: C3, 60, 75, 81, 85, 87, 175 • Tram: 3

Bas reliefs depicting Constantine adorn his triumphal arch.

Arco di Costantino

Emperor Constantine built his triumphal arch, the Arco di Costantino, in A.D. 315 to commemorate his victory over Emperor Maxentius in a civil war. The triple arcade is a traditional approach to victory architecture, but Constantine's choice of decoration is revolutionary. Rather than having new reliefs made from scratch, Constantine plundered the carvings on monuments to Emperors Trajan, Hadrian, and Marcus Aurelius and added them to his own arch. In all cases, his own face was carved onto their bodies. The panels show Constantine fulfilling the imperial virtues of virility and pagan piety. On the southwest side, the relief panel on the top right originally showed Marcus Aurelius making an animal and wine sacrifice; the image now shows **Constantine in the act of pagan veneration.** The few examples of fourth-century works that appear on the arch employ stocky proportions and odd scale, iconography that marks a clear departure from the classical realism of other images. The band over the small arch on the southwest side depicts soldiers attacking a city wall that is barely taller than they are.

Piazza del Colosseo • Metro: Colosseo, Line B • Bus: C3, 60, 75, 81, 85, 87, 175 • Tram: 3

Santi Giovanni e Paolo

The 12th-century church commemorates two Roman officers, Giovanni (John) and Paolo (Paul), who converted to Christianity under Emperor Constantine. They were beheaded for refusing to fight on behalf of the pagan emperor Julian, known as "the Apostate." The church underwent radical decorative changes between the 17th and 20th centuries, which saw the addition of dozens of funeral chapels and funerary monuments for nobles and clergy. Off the right aisle, a large **domed chapel** from the mid-19th century houses the relics of St. Paul of the Cross, founder of the Passionists, a Roman Catholic religious order. The **crystal chandeliers** in the nave, donated by the Waldorf Astoria Hotel in New York City, are the most recent addition—the gift was coordinated by Francis Spellman, Archbishop of New York, in the 1940s. Beneath Santi Giovanni e Paolo lie the remains of two Roman buildings—a multistory apartment building and a three-story villa—embellished with mosaics, frescoes, and fountains. These two buildings, the **Case Romane al Celio** (*Clivo di Scauro, www.caseromane.it, 06 7045 4544, €€, closed Tues. and Wed.*), were

The ornate baroque interior of Santi Giovanni e Paolo makes an ideal backdrop for a wedding.

unified into a single-family home in the fourth century. According to tradition, John and Paul lived here and were buried in the house after their martyrdom. The site became a place of pilgrimage and the location of a church around A.D. 395. The ancient rooms lay sealed off and forgotten until their rediscovery in the late 19th century.

Piazza dei Santi Giovanni e Paolo 13 • 06 700 5745 • Metro: Circo Massimo, Colosseo, Line B • Bus: 60, 75, 81, 175, 673

Santo Stefano Rotondo

4 St. Stephen, the first Christian martyr, was stoned to death for his faith around A.D. 35 in Jerusalem. The fifth-century church that bears his name is formed of two concentric rings divided by recycled marble and granite columns from Roman and early Christian buildings. Its open, luminous, and airy interior

A mosaic in the apse of a chapel at Santo Stefano Rotondo depicts Sts. Primo and Feliciano.

contrasts starkly with the subject of the **pastel frescoes** on the walls: 34 gory scenes of martyrdom painted by Antonio Tempesta and Niccolò Pomarancio for Pope Gregory XIII in the late 16th century. In a side chapel to the left of the main entrance, an altar is embellished with **sixth-century mosaics** showing Sts. Primo and Feliciano flanking a bejeweled cross. Outside, the **gardens** offer shady respite from the city heat.

Via Santo Stefano Rotondo 7 • www.060608.it • 06 421 199 • Closed Sun. p.m. and Mon. • Metro: Colosseo, Line B • Bus: 81, 117, 673

Santi Quattro Coronati

5 The church of Santi Quattro Coronati (literally, Four Crowned Martyrs) honors four unnamed Christians killed for refusing to worship the pagan god Aesculapius. The severe Romanesque style of the fortress-like and forbidding brick exterior continues in the dark and somber interior. Find relief from the gloom in the 12th-century **cloister**—a tranquil arrangement of columns built around a lovely garden. Frescoes in the 13th-century oratory of **San Silvestro** *(open early morning and late afternoon)* depict the stories of Pope Silvester I and Emperor Constantine. The images are flat and reminiscent of Byzantine art. They were painted before Renaissance art concepts, already stirring in Florence, had fully taken hold in Rome.

Via dei Querceti • www.santiquattrocoronati.org • Metro: Colosseo, Line B • Bus: C3, 60, 75, 81, 85, 87, 175, 673

San Clemente

6 The medieval church of San Clemente preserves a magnificent **gold and glass mosaic** in its apse (see p. 112), a brilliantly executed **mosaic floor,** and a **tranquil courtyard,** all from the 12th century. The church, which is under the care of Irish Dominicans, is dedicated to St. Clement, the fourth pope. According to tradition he was martyred by being tossed into the sea with an anchor around

COLOSSEO TO SAN PIETRO IN VINCOLI

his neck; the anchor now embellishes the church as a reminder of his sacrifice. A chapel to the left of the main entrance depicts more scenes of martyrdom: **the life and death of St. Catherine.** The frescoes were painted in the mid-15th century by either one of the Renaissance masters Masaccio or Masolino, or perhaps by both. Beneath the church, the **original church** of San Clemente, built in the late fourth and early fifth centuries, is open to visitors (see p. 70). To reach the archaeological site, purchase a ticket in the office off the church's right aisle. A staircase leads into the lower church, which was filled in with earth around 1100 and used as a foundation for the upper church. A staircase from the end of the left aisle leads down to a more ancient level consisting of **two late first-century Roman buildings.** The first was an apartment building, containing a sanctuary to the Persian god Mithras. The second was a public structure, perhaps a warehouse or mint.

Via di San Giovanni in Laterano 108 • www.basilicasan clemente.com • 06 774 0021 • Excavations: € • Closed Sun. a.m. • Metro: Colosseo, Line B • Bus: C3, 60, 75, 81, 85, 87, 175, 673

GOOD **EATS**

■ **LI RIONI**
Near the Colosseo, delicious thin and crispy pizzas are made in a wood-fired oven. Dinner only. **Via Santi Quattro Coronati 24, 06 7045 0605, €€**

■ **TAVERNA DEI QUARANTA**
Outdoor tables on the Via Claudia, near Santi Giovanni e Paolo, make this simple trattoria a pleasant place to refuel with a plate of pasta. **Via Claudia 24, 06 700 0550, €€**

■ **TEMPIO DI ISIDE**
This fish-only restaurant a short walk from San Clemente offers some of the city's freshest catch skillfully and creatively prepared. **Via Pietro Verri 11, 06 700 4741, €€€–€€€€**

San Pietro in Vincoli

7 Originally consecrated in 439, the church owes much of its current decoration to the 15th and 16th centuries. The church was under the guardianship of Cardinal Giuliano della Rovere (elected Pope Julius II in 1503), who commissioned Michelangelo to design his tomb. Although he intended his massive **funerary monument** to be placed in the Basilica di San Pietro (St. Peter's Basilica; see pp. 135–136), a series of political and financial problems led the incomplete structure to be installed in San Pietro in Vincoli decades after the pope's death. The tomb's protagonist, Moses, sits transfixed on a throne, fingers tangled in his beard, the tablets bearing the Ten Commandments tucked under his right arm. It is perhaps Michelangelo's most powerful sculpture and seems full of life despite its cold marble medium. In niches on either side of Moses stand Jacob's wives, Leah and Rachel. The church is named for the chains *(vincoli)* that bound St. Peter in Rome and Jerusalem. Legend holds that when the two chains were brought together in the fifth century, they miraculously fused. You can see the chains in a glass reliquary beneath the main altar, and the large ceiling painting of 1706 by Giovanni Battista Parodi depicts the **miracle of the chains.** To the left of the main entrance, a 15th-century fresco shows a procession of penitents praying for an end to the plague.

Piazza San Pietro in Vincoli • www.060608.it • 06 9784 4950 • Metro: Cavour, Colosseo, Line B • Bus: 75, 84

IN THE **KNOW**

Michelangelo's sculpture of Moses in San Pietro in Vincoli captures a moment of high emotion. The Bible tells how, after Moses had received the Ten Commandments, he found his people worshiping a golden calf. Furious, he burned the idol, ground it into powder, and made his people drink it with water.

Michelangelo's statue of Moses adorns the tomb of Pope Julius II in San Pietro in Vincoli.

Colosseo

Supreme among Roman amphitheaters, the first-century Colosseo was a venue for epic entertainment and bloody games.

Crowds up to 60,000 strong filled the tiers, shaded from the sun by a rigging of awnings.

Construction of the Colosseo (Colosseum) began in A.D. 72 under Emperor Vespasian. Eight years later it was inaugurated by his son, Titus. Named the Flavian Amphitheater for this imperial family, the theater took on the moniker Colosseo in the Middle Ages due to its proximity to a colossal 115-foot-tall (35 m) statue of Emperor Nero. After the fall of the Roman Empire—and more than 450 years of wild-beast hunts, executions, and gladiatorial combat—the Colosseo's arcades were filled with hovels, stables, and fortresses, and its stones were pillaged.

OUTER WALLS

First stroll around the Colosseo's exterior. The preserved northern side consists of four levels of arcades utilizing different **column styles:** sturdy Tuscan at the lowest level, scroll-like Ionic at the next, and more elaborate Corinthian at the top two levels. There were 80 **entrance arches** leading inside before the southern walls collapsed—their outline is traced by a white line in the sidewalk. The surviving arches bear **Roman numeral inscriptions,** which corresponded to those on the spectators' tickets. The limestone blocks were quarried 20 miles (32 km) east of Rome at Tivoli.

THE CROSS

Inside the arena, the elliptical structure stands 160 feet tall (49 m), 660 feet long (200 m), and 540 feet wide (165 m). A **bronze cross** at the north end of the stage's short axis dates from 1900. It was erected to honor Christians allegedly martyred here.

SUBTERRANEAN STRUCTURE

In the center of the arena, four parallel walls are exposed that formed part of

SAVVY **TRAVELER**

Beat the crowds at the Colosseo by buying tickets online or by phone *(www .pierreci.it, 06 3996 7700)*. A booking fee is added on, but tickets also cover entry to the Foro Romano and Palatino.

the 20-foot-deep (6 m) **substructure.** Originally this "basement" was covered with wooden flooring topped with a 4-inch (10 cm) layer of sand. The substructure acted like the backstage of a theater. Caged animals, condemned criminals, gladiators, and props were kept here before being brought onstage. Vertical shafts inside the walls allowed the animal cages to be winched up to arena level. The beasts emerged through trap doors in the wooden floor.

ENGINEERING EXHIBIT

A small display on the second floor focuses on the substructure's original engineering. Models and artists' renderings re-create the simple lift mechanisms and limestone weights discovered during excavations. Animal remains are also on display.

COLOSSEO TO SAN PIETRO IN VINCOLI

Piazza del Colosseo • www.060608.it • 06 3996 7700 • Ticket offices: Piazza del Colosseo, Via di San Gregorio, Largo Salaria Vecchia • €€€ • Closed Jan. 1 and Dec. 25 • Metro: Colosseo, Line B • Bus: C3, 60, 75, 81, 85, 87, 175 • Tram: 3

Bread & Circuses

Roman emperors knew how to keep their citizens loyal and content: Subsidize their food and lay on lavish quantities of free entertainment—*panis et circenses* (bread and games), as the poet Juvenal referred to these freebies around A.D. 100. Games such as chariot races and athletics championships took place in open-air arenas called circuses. The emperors or other wealthy citizens financed them, as well as sponsoring the baths where people could socialize and be pampered.

Emperor Vespasian initiated the building of the Colosseo (above). A second-century A.D. Roman fresco depicts a gladiator in combat with a lion in the arena (right).

Blood Sports

With its marble columns, silk cushions, fountains, vast awning, and room for an audience of 60,000, the Colosseo (see pp. 66–67) was the greatest monument to this culture of indulging the citizens. Emperor Titus launched it in A.D. 80 with a festival lasting 100 days during which scores of gladiators and some 5,000 exotic animals fought and died before an audience drawn from all over the empire.

The biggest chariot-racing stadium was the Circo Massimo (see pp. 166–167), the remains of which can still be traced between the Aventine and Palatine hills. It could hold 250,000 spectators, a quarter of the city's population. In A.D. 85, Emperor Domitian built a smaller stadium for 30,000, to stage athletics in the nude Greek style. Gladiatorial combats and executions were also held here, in what is now the Piazza Navona (see p. 123). Rome's last stadium to be built (A.D. 309) is the best preserved: the Circo di Massenzio on the Via Appia (in the southern suburbs), where 18,000 spectators could watch chariots tear around the circuit.

COLOSSEO TO SAN PIETRO IN VINCOLI

Bath Time

The Romans turned bathing into a fine art. The public baths were like leisure centers: places to relax and get clean, exercise, have a massage, meet friends, play dice and board games, and eat a snack. The Terme di Caracalla (Baths of Caracalla, see pp. 167–168), begun in A.D. 211, were the best in the empire and continued in use until the sixth century. Today the ruins show their scale—they were big enough to take 1,600 bathers at a time—but they only hint at the luxurious tiled and decorated interior that lay within. The complex included a gymnasium, shops, gardens dotted with sculptures, libraries, and concert halls. The cost of entry was minimal, or even free on days (sometimes entire years) when a sponsor was paying.

LOST **PLEASURES**

Only traces of these baths and circus remain:

Circus Vaticanus Emperor Nero developed this circus by the Basilica di San Pietro for his Olympic-style games.

Terme di Agrippa General Agrippa established the first public bath complex in Rome, near the Pantheon, circa 20 B.C.

Terme di Diocleziano Diocletian built Rome's largest baths (see pp. 76–77) in A.D. 298 near Piazza della Repubblica.

Terme di Traiano Substantial chunks of Trajan's huge set of baths, dating to A.D. 104–109, survive in the Colle Oppio park near the Colosseo.

Underground Rome

Rome is a city of layers in which ancient ruins are trapped beneath medieval buildings, which in turn form the foundation of the visible city. Excavations have revealed the city's urban stratification and uncovered buildings that had been filled in with rubble and earth—the effect of time and the elements.

■ SAN CLEMENTE

San Clemente (see pp. 63–64) is perhaps the best site for enjoying Rome's many layers. Enter the 12th-century church, then head downstairs to the fourth-century predecessor and, below that, to a first-century A.D. Roman apartment building, 30 feet (9 m) below modern ground level. Here a sanctuary is dedicated to the Persian god Mithras, a popular deity in Rome, whose worship rivaled Christianity. Stone benches line the walls, and a relief on the altar depicts the god slaying a bull.

Via di San Giovanni in Laterano 108 • www .basilicasanclemente.com • 06 774 0021 • Excavations: € • Closed Sun. a.m. • Metro: Colosseo, Line B • Bus: C3, 60, 75, 81, 85, 87, 175, 673

■ AREA ARCHEOLOGICA VICUS CAPRARIUS

Renovations of Cinema Trevi near the Fontana di Trevi (see p. 92)

turned up a wall from the first century A.D. Further digs uncovered two Roman buildings—a water tower and apartment block—both of which were abandoned in the fifth century. The ancient remains lie 27 feet (8 m) below modern ground level. Visit **Harry's Bar** in the Mondadori bookshop on ground level and take a peek at the ruins through the Plexiglas floor, then head beneath the bar and cinema for a walk through them.

Harry's Bar, Mondadori, Vicolo del Puttarello 25 • 06 474 2103 • Metro: Barberini, Line A or Cavour, Colosseo, Line B • Bus: C3, 52, 53, 61, 62, 63, 71, 80, 95, 116, 119, 175, 492, 590

■ DOMUS ROMANE

Just steps away from the bustling Piazza Venezia, the remains of two lavishly decorated Roman villas lie beneath a Renaissance palace. The noble homes, which were uncovered in 2007 and opened to the public in

St. Peter is purportedly buried along with 146 other popes in the crypt beneath St. Peter's.

2010, preserve elaborate mosaic floors, marble wall veneer, and evidence of plumbing and baths. The visit begins with a multimedia presentation. Throughout the site, visual effects recreate the buildings and spotlight elements of Roman domesticity.

Palazzo Valentini, Via IV Novembre 119/A • www.palazzovalentini.it • 06 32810 • €€ • Tours in English once a day, reservation required • Closed Tues., Jan. 1, May 1, and Dec. 25 • Metro: Barberini, Line A or Cavour, Colosseo, Line B • Bus: 40, 60, 64, 70, 170

■ Scavi di San Pietro
Buried 30 feet (9 m) beneath the Basilica di San Pietro (St. Peter's

Basilica; see pp. 135–136) lies a cemetery from Roman times. A visit underground begins in a pagan necropolis, where brick mausoleums stand along an ancient road. The tombs preserve stucco, marble, and mosaic work. The tour passes a tomb supposed to be that of St. Peter. Vatican authorities claim the apostle's relics were discovered here in the mid-20th century.

Piazza San Pietro, Vatican City • www.vatican.va • 06 6988 5318 • Advance booking reservation required: e-mail scavi@fsp.va or fax 06 6987 3017 (children under 15 not permitted) • €€€ • Closed Sun. and public holidays • Metro: Ottaviano, Line A • Bus: 19, 23, 32, 34, 40, 49, 81, 62, 492, 982, 990

Laterano to Terme di Diocleziano

The upper slopes of the Quirinal, Viminal, Esquiline, and Caelian Hills make for an interesting ramble into Rome's Catholic art and architecture. Two of Rome's most important pilgrimage sites mingle with the city's greatest collection of ancient frescoes in the museum of Palazzo Massimo alle Terme. The zone covers every major art historical period, from antiquity to modernity, and it has a number of splendid monuments. In spite of their importance, the area remains firmly off the tourist beat, and visitors will likely encounter more locals and pilgrims than outsiders. A visit begins at a baroque church on Via XX Settembre that commemorates the day Garibaldi's troops stormed the city in 1870, an event that would culminate in the unification of Italy.

◖ Nuns kneel at their devotions in San Giovanni in Laterano, the cathedral of Rome.

NEIGHBORHOOD **WALK**

1 **Santa Maria della Vittoria** (see p. 76)
Beside a busy intersection, a limestone church facade gives way to an opulent baroque church that draws visitors for its chapel by Gian Lorenzo Bernini. Take Via Vittorio Emanuele Orlando southeast to Piazza della Repubblica.

2 **Terme di Diocleziano** (see pp. 76–77)
Behind a curving brick wall, the Baths of Diocletian, now a church, open into a dramatic vertical space transformed by Michelangelo. From Piazza della Repubblica take Via delle Terme di Diocleziano southeast to Largo di Villa Peretti.

3 **Palazzo Massimo alle Terme** (see pp. 80–81)
The museum holds some of antiquity's best preserved mosaics and frescoes, as well as an impressive sculpture collection. Turn left out of the museum and take Via del Viminale to the end. Turn left onto Via A. Depretis and walk four blocks southeast.

4 **Santa Maria Maggiore** (see p. 78)
This top pilgrimage site is reputed to contain the relics of Jesus' manger. From Piazza Santa Maria Maggiore, take Via Santa Prassede and enter through Santa Prassede's side door.

5 **Santa Prassede** (see p. 78)
The church contains some of Rome's most spectacular mosaics from the early Christian era, as well as a glimmering 12th-century apse. Backtrack to Piazza Santa Maria Maggiore, and follow Via Merulana south to Piazza San Giovanni in Laterano.

6 **San Giovanni in Laterano** (see pp. 78–79)
Rome's cathedral has been built and rebuilt several times, resulting in a mixture of styles. Exit through the front door and take Via Carlo Felice seven blocks to the church of Santa Croce in Gerusalemme.

**LATERANO TO TERME DI DIOCLEZIANO   DISTANCE: 2.7 MILES (4.3 KM)
TIME: APPROX. 5 HOURS   METRO START: REPPUBLICA, BARBERINI, LINE A**

LATERANO TO TERME DI DIOCLEZIANO

Map labels:
Santa Maria della Vittoria
Repubblica
PIAZZA D. REPUBBLICA
Terme di Diocleziano
Palazzo Massimo alle Terme (Museo Nazionale Romano)
Termini
PIAZZA DELL' ESQUILINO
PIAZZA SANTA MARIA MAGGIORE
Santa Maria Maggiore
Santa Prassede
Cavour
VIA G. LANZA
VIA CAVOUR
VIA NAZIONALE
VIMINALE
VIA DEPRETIS
SETTEMBRE
XX
VIA CERNAIA

Laterano to
Terme di Diocleziano

The meandering pathway hits numerous baroque masterpieces,
a transformed bathing complex, and important pilgrimage destinations.

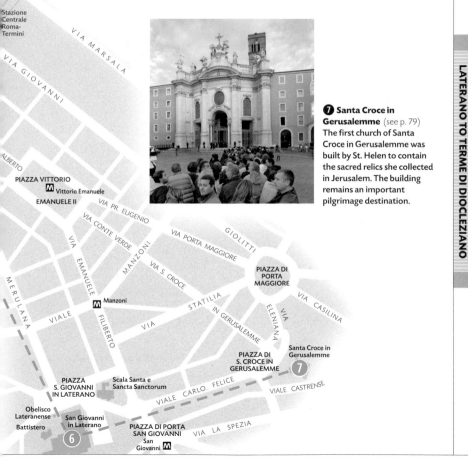

❼ Santa Croce in Gerusalemme (see p. 79) The first church of Santa Croce in Gerusalemme was built by St. Helen to contain the sacred relics she collected in Jerusalem. The building remains an important pilgrimage destination.

Santa Maria della Vittoria

1 An explosion of baroque exuberance greets you as you step inside Santa Maria della Vittoria (Our Lady of Victory). Cardinal Scipione Borghese, the creator of the Villa Borghese (see pp. 107–109), built the church between 1608 and 1620. Swathes of stucco and gilding adorn the interior. But the church's main draw is the **Cornaro Chapel** located at the end of the left aisle. Designed by Gian Lorenzo Bernini in the 1660s, its centerpiece is his sculpture, the **"Ecstasy of St. Teresa,"** depicting the Spanish mystic and monastic reformer, St. Teresa of Avila, reclining on a cloud, as an angel prepares to plunge an arrow into her heart. Her back is arched and her facial expression implies physical ecstasy, conflating sensual pleasure and spiritual enlightenment. The Cornaro family is portrayed in low relief in theater boxes on opposing sides of the chapel.

Via XX Settembre 17 • 06 4274 0571 • Metro: Repubblica or Barberini, Line A • Bus: 60, 62, 84, 175

GOOD **EATS**

■ CONTER
This small café and bistro near San Giovanni in Laterano serves drinks and light snacks and hosts a popular *aperitivo* happy hour. **Piazza San Giovanni in Laterano 64, €**

■ DA DANILO
Danilo Valente works the front of the house of a trattoria near Piazza Vittorio Emanuele II, while his mother prepares classic Roman dishes. The carbonara and *cacio e pepe* are among the best in town. **Via Petrarca 13, 06 7720 0111, €€€**

■ TRATTORIA MONTI
A long-established family-run business not far from Santa Maria Maggiore, the trattoria serves thoughtfully prepared dishes, including fish and game, from Italy's Le Marche region. **Via di San Vito 13a, 06 446 6573, €€€**

Terme di Diocleziano

2 Construction of the Baths of Diocletian began in A.D. 298 during that emperor's reign, and finished in 306 under Constantius. The large public bathing complex sprawled across the crest of the Quirinale and was among the grandest structures of late antiquity. In the 1560s, Michelangelo transformed part of the ruins into the church of **Santa Maria degli Angeli e dei Martiri** (*Piazza delle Repubblica and Via Cernaia 9, www.santamariadegliangeliroma.it, 06 488 0812*). The church's interior is awash with Christian imagery, but its height and eight Egyptian granite columns testify to the building's original secular

The Museo Nazionale Romano at the Terme di Diocleziano includes pagan Roman sculptures.

purpose. On the eastern side of the complex, a **Carthusian cloister** designed by Michelangelo now contains one of the collections of the **Museo Nazionale Romano,** which includes hundreds of ancient Roman statues, reliefs, and sarcophagi.

Piazza della Repubblica and Via Enrico de Nicola 79 • www.archeoroma.beniculturali .it/en/museums/national-roman-museum-baths-diocletian • 06 3996 7700 • €€ • Closed Mon., Jan. 1, May 1, and Dec. 25 • Metro: Repubblica, Line A, or Termini, Lines A and B • Bus: 40, 60, 62, 64, 84, 175

Palazzo Massimo alle Terme

3 See pp. 80–81.

Largo di Villa Peretti 1• www.archeoroma.beniculturali.it/en/museums/ national-roman-museum-palazzo-massimo-alle-terme • 06 3996 7700 • €€ • Closed Mon., Jan. 1, May 1, and Dec. 25 • Metro: Termini, Lines A and B • Bus: 40, 60, 64, 75, 84 • Tram: 5, 14

Santa Maria Maggiore

4 The original church of Santa Maria Maggiore was built on the crest of the Esquiline Hill after a supposedly miraculous snowfall occurred there in August of A.D. 356. During the Middle Ages, the church received extensive renovations. According to tradition, its ceiling is gilded with gold from the New World gifted to the pope by Queen Isabella of Spain. Santa Maria Maggiore became the final resting spot of numerous members of the Roman nobility and of the sculptor and architect Gian Lorenzo Bernini, whose tomb lies near the end of the right aisle. Nearby, the **Cappella Sistina,** a chapel built by Sixtus V, houses the 16th-century pope's massive marble funeral monument.

Piazza di Santa Maria Maggiore • www.vatican.va /various/ basiliche/sm_maggiore/index_en.html • 06 6988 6800 • Metro: Termini, Lines A and B • Bus: 70, 75, 84 • Tram: 5, 14

SAVVY **TRAVELER**

The miraculous snowfall that led to the building of Santa Maria Maggiore on the Esquiline Hill is celebrated each year in the feast of Our Lady of Snows. On August 5, locals gather for celebrations, during which they throw white rose petals from a gallery around the church's dome.

Santa Prassede

5 Often overlooked by visitors, the church of St. Prassede offers a feast of medieval art and architecture. The current church dates from around A.D. 820. Mosaics in the **St. Zeno Chapel** off the right aisle depict Christ, the Virgin, and saints in the Byzantine style, a rarity for Rome. The apse mosaic shows Christ flanked by saints, including the church's patron, the ninth-century Pope Paschal I, who holds a model of the building. Beneath the main altar, ancient marble sarchophagi contain the relics of St. Prassede and her sister, St. Pudenziana.

Via di Santa Prassede 9a • 06 488 2456 • Metro: Termini, Lines A and B • Bus: 70, 75, 84 • Tram: 5, 14

San Giovanni in Laterano

6 Contrary to popular belief, St. Peter's Basilica is not Rome's cathedral. That title rests with St. John Lateran, which has been the seat of the bishop of Rome (who is also the pope) since the fourth century. Emperor Constantine built it as Rome's first Christian basilica on land confiscated from the Laterani family. Until the 14th century, it formed part of a massive estate where the popes lived and the papal court congregated. Enter through the magnificent east porch, whose doors were taken from the Foro Romano in 1660 by order of Pope Alexander VII. Francesco Borromini was largely responsible for the 17th-century remodeling and design of the interior. At the intersection of the nave and transept, the **ciborium** (altar canopy) contains relics of St. Peter and St. Paul, whose skulls lie within the golden busts on the monument. The transept is richly decorated with **16th-century mannerist paintings** by Cavalier d'Arpino, Orazio Gentileschi, and Cesare Nebbia. From the transept, visit the serene **12th-century cloister,** with twin twisted columns and inlaid mosaics.

Piazza San Giovanni in Laterano • www.vatican.va/various/basiliche/san_giovanni/ vr_tour/index-en.html • 06 6988 6392 • Metro: San Giovanni, Line A • Bus: 81, 85, 87, 571 • Tram: 3

Santa Croce in Gerusalemme

7 St. Helen, mother of Emperor Constantine, built the original church of Santa Croce in Gerusalemme (Holy Cross in Jerusalem) around A.D. 320. It stood on her own property to house supposed relics of Christ's cross that she found on Mount Calvary during a pilgrimage to Jerusalem. The current church is a subsequent rebuilding, but the relics survive. At the end of the left aisle, a staircase leads to the **Cappella delle Reliquie** (Chapel of the Relics), which contains St. Helen's remnants of the cross along with other similar treasures, including two supposed thorns from Jesus' crown of thorns.

Piazza di Santa Croce in Gerusalemme 12 • www.santa croceroma.it • 06 7061 3053 • Metro: San Giovanni, Line A • Bus: 571 • Tram: 3, 5, 14

The ornate 14th-century Gothic ciborium covering the high altar of San Giovanni in Laterano contrasts with the baroque style of the rest of the interior.

Palazzo Massimo alle Terme

Bronze, marble, and fresco masterpieces mingle in one of the world's most impressive collections of antiquities.

Frescoes from the Villa Livia depict a surprising variety of trees and plants in flower and fruit.

Considering the sheer number of collections in Rome, prioritizing can present a challenge. For visitors interested in ancient frescoes, however, a visit to the Palazzo Massimo alle Terme is a must. The 19th-century neoclassical building became one of Rome's four national museums in 1998 and is home to spectacular wall paintings detached from republican- and imperial-era villas in Rome and its suburbs. The halls also show off phenomenal sculpture and bronze works, as well as a fine collection of mosaics.

■ First Emperor

A standout among the portraits of emperors is the late first-century B.C. statue on the first floor depicting **Augustus as Pontifex Maximus** (high priest). Augustus, with his signature good looks, wears a robe with heavy drapery, the symbol of piety and priesthood.

■ Classical Sculpture

A bronze statue of a **"Boxer at Rest"** portrays a seated boxer, exhausted and battered, his face showing signs of injury and age. Created by a Greek sculptor probably working in the second century B.C., this deeply moving work of art seems to express real compassion for the subject. Other highlights include Roman copies of earlier Greek originals, among them the **"Discus Thrower,"** a model of athletic perfection, and the **"Sleeping Hermaphrodite."**

■ Bronze Ship Fittings

The third emperor, Caligula, built lavishly decorated yachts at Lake Nemi, near Rome. The boats were apparently sunk after Caligula's assassination and excavated by Mussolini. The digs, which involved draining the lake, turned up elaborate bronze fittings depicting wolves and mythological figures.

■ Portonaccio Sarcophagus

A large **marble casket,** found off the Via Tiburtina in eastern Rome and carved circa A.D. 180, brilliantly portrays a furious battle between Romans and barbarians. It was made for Aulus Iulius Pompilius, who served under Emperor Marcus Aurelius in military campaigns in Germany.

■ Frescoes

Vibrant wall paintings from the **Villa Livia** at Prima Porta and the **Villa Farnesina** in Trastevere are on show on the second floor. Frescoes from the Villa Livia's *triclinium* (dining room) represent pines, oaks, fruit trees, and local flowers in the earliest example of continuous garden painting, circa 35 B.C.

SAVVY **TRAVELER**

Take a guided tour of the ancient frescoes so you don't miss out on any of the details or historical context. Reserve in advance by phone: 06 3996 7700.

LATERANO TO TERME DI DIOCLEZIANO

Largo di Villa Peretti 1 • www.archeoroma.beniculturali.it/en/museums/national-roman-museum-palazzo-massimo-alle-terme • 06 3996 7700 • €€ • Closed Mon., Jan. 1, May 1, and Dec. 25 • Metro: Termini, Lines A and B • Bus: 40, 60, 64, 75, 84 • Tram: 5, 14

Baroque City

The baroque style of the 17th century, typified by high emotion, dynamic movement, and grandeur, found an ideal outlet in Rome. Under papal patronage, the greatest sculptors and architects of the day transformed the face of the city for all time with ornate churches, statuary, and squares. Supreme among these artists were Gian Lorenzo Bernini, a man of exceptional gifts who made his first sculpture at age 11, and Francesco Borromini.

Light from an overhead window filters down on Bernini's dramatic "Ecstasy of St. Teresa" (above). Borromini began embellishing the interior of San Giovanni in Laterano in 1646 (right).

Papal Architect

In 1629, Pope Urban VIII, of the powerful Barberini family, appointed Bernini to decorate the interior of the newly finished **Basilica di San Pietro** (see pp. 135–136). Here, Bernini left an indelibly baroque mark upon Carlo Maderno's basilica with features that include the great bronze canopy, or baldacchino, over the altar, a huge marble statue of Longinus for one of the piers supporting the dome, and a bronze and marble tomb for Urban. To reach the basilica, visitors cross Bernini's gigantic yet graceful baroque **Piazza San Pietro** (see pp. 134–135), a great architectural achievement and a symbol of the city.

Elsewhere, Bernini's works include the famed **"Ecstasy of St. Teresa"** in **Santa Maria della Vittoria** (see p. 76)—a superb example of his prowess at turning marble into a seemingly fluid, living form. The sculpture reveals a prime motive behind the baroque—the Catholic Church's crusade to challenge the Protestant Reformation. The vigor and emotional intensity of such art thus implied the supreme importance of pope and church.

Genius of Borromini

Just a year younger than Bernini, the Swiss-born Borromini's first solo work was the church of **San Carlo alle Quattro Fontane** (see p. 90). The church's undulating facade remains a perfect expression of the inspiring energy of the baroque. Later commissions included Borromini's work on the churches of **Sant'Agnese in Agone** (see p. 123) and **San Giovanni in Laterano** (see pp. 78–79). Another Borromini masterpiece is **Sant'Ivo alla Sapienza**—tucked away east of Piazza Navona—whose features include a star-shaped design, curving walls, and a cupola topped with a corkscrew-like spiral. More erratic in temperament than his urbane rival, Bernini, Borromini took his own life in 1667.

SMALL **CHURCHES**

Some baroque churches are tiny—rather than grand—masterpieces, not to be missed.

San Carlo alle Quattro Fontane, on the Quirinale (see p. 90)—Borromini created an architectural gem that could fit inside one of the four great pilasters of St. Peter's.

Sant'Andrea al Quirinale, also on the Quirinal Hill (see pp. 90–91)—For architect Bernini this was a labor of love for which he refused to accept payment.

Sant'Ivo alla Sapienza, between the Pantheon and Piazza Navona—Borromini designed this as the chapel to the University of Rome.

LATERANO TO TERME DI DIOCLEZIANO

Obelisks

In ancient Egypt, granite monoliths, often inscribed with hieroglyphics, stood on either side of the entrances to temples. The first of these obelisks came to Rome in the first century B.C. as war trophies after Augustus's conquest of Egypt. In all, eight originals survive in the city, while five others are Roman imitations.

■ PIAZZA SAN GIOVANNI IN LATERANO
Carved from Aswan granite, Rome's oldest Egyptian obelisk dates to circa 1400 B.C. and originally stood at Karnak on the banks of the Nile. In A.D. 357, Emperor Constantine II brought it to Rome to adorn the Circo Massimo (see pp. 166–167), where, with the passage of time, it fell, broke into three pieces, and lay buried beneath flood deposit and debris. It was uncovered once more in the 1580s under Pope Sixtus V, who had it restored and moved to Piazza San Giovanni in Laterano.

■ PIAZZA DEL POPOLO
Emperor Augustus brought the 14th-century B.C. obelisk to Rome in 10 B.C. to celebrate the 40th anniversary of his conquest of Egypt. Its first Roman home was in the Circo Massimo. Pope Sixtus V moved it to its current location in 1589.

■ PIAZZA TRINITÀ DEI MONTI
Situated at the top of the Spanish Steps, the "Sallustian obelisk" is an Egyptian-inspired Roman design that was probably built as decoration for the hippodrome circa A.D. 270.

■ PIAZZA NAVONA
This Roman copy of an Egyptian obelisk has stood in three different locations. Emperor Domitian commissioned it in the first century A.D. for a temple to the Egyptian god Serapis on the Quirinale. In the fourth century, Emperor Maxentius moved it to his circus on the Via Appia (see p. 68). In 1648, Pope Innocent X transferred it to Piazza Navona to be the focal point of Bernini's Fontana dei Quattro Fiumi.

■ PIAZZA DELLA MINERVA
In front of the Church of Santa Maria sopra Minerva, a small sixth-century B.C.

LATERANO TO TERME DI DIOCLEZIANO

obelisk of Aswan granite sits atop a white marble elephant designed by Bernini. Emperor Domitian brought the obelisk to Rome in the first century. In 1655, it was rediscovered on the site of the Iseum, a nearby sanctuary dedicated to the Egyptian goddess Isis.

■ PIAZZA DEL PARLAMENTO

Pharaoh Psammetichus II commissioned this 102-foot-tall (31m) obelisk in the sixth century B.C. Emperor Augustus moved it to Rome in 10 B.C. to be the centerpiece of his Horologium Augusti (sundial of Augustus). Pope Pius VI had it restored and reerected in front of the Palazzo Montecitorio in 1792.

■ PIAZZA SAN PIETRO

Tradition holds that St. Peter was martyred near this obelisk circa A.D. 67. Egyptian-made, but for the Romans, it originally stood in Alexandria. Emperor Caligula brought it to Rome in A.D. 37 to adorn the Circus Vaticanus (see p. 69). It remained standing during the Middle Ages. In 1585, Pope Sixtus V moved it several yards, so it would be centered in front of the Basilica di San Pietro when the facade was completed.

The obelisk in Piazza del Popolo once stood in Egypt's third major city, Heliopolis.

The Quirinale to Via Veneto

The Quirinale—Rome's tallest hill—has always been a political heartland. Ministries and foreign embassies flank the arrow-straight thoroughfare of Via XX Settembre, which leads from Rome's northeastern gate to the Palazzo del Quirinale (Quirinal Palace). Yet, to wander the streets and squares of the Quirinal Hill is to experience the intensity of 17th-century—rather than modern—political life. Baroque palaces and churches filled with precious artworks express the power and wealth of that era's dominant political faction: the Church. The popes moved to the Quirinale from their insalubrious riverside abode at St. Peter's in the late 1500s, and ruled from the Palazzo del Quirinale until the unification of Italy forced them back to the Vatican in 1870. The kings of Italy then occupied the palace until 1946, when it became the seat of the president.

◑ Niccolò Salvi's Fontana di Trevi, described by Charles Dickens as "a silvery sight to the eye and ear"

The Quirinale to Via Veneto

Stunning views of Rome combine with fine baroque architecture and a stroll along the city's most famous thoroughfare.

❾ Via Veneto
(see p. 93) Enjoy a coffee or an aperitif on the road that was once synonymous with *la dolce vita*.

❽ Santa Maria della Concezione dei Cappuccini (see pp. 92–93) Confront mortality in the extraordinary crypt of this church, before meandering up the Via Veneto.

❼ Palazzo Barberini (see pp. 94–95) After admiring works of the Italian masters in this magnificent palace, head to the southern end of Via Veneto.

❻ Fontana di Trevi (see p. 92) Take a break and enjoy the sheer audacity of Roman architecture. Then move up, away from the crowds to the Piazza Barberini.

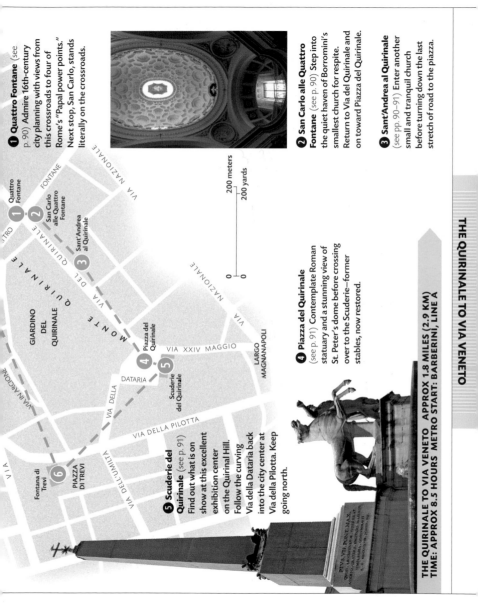

1 Quattro Fontane (see p. 90) Admire 16th-century city planning with views from this crossroads to four of Rome's "Papal power points." Next stop, San Carlo, stands literally on the crossroads.

2 San Carlo alle Quattro Fontane (see p. 90) Step into the quiet haven of Borromini's smallest church for respite. Return to Via del Quirinale and on toward Piazza del Quirinale.

3 Sant'Andrea al Quirinale (see pp. 90–91) Enter another small and tranquil church before turning down the last stretch of road to the piazza.

4 Piazza del Quirinale (see p. 91) Contemplate Roman statuary and a stunning view of St. Peter's dome before crossing over to the Scuderie—former stables, now restored.

5 Scuderie del Quirinale (see p. 91) Find out what is on show at this excellent exhibition center on the Quirinal Hill. Follow the curving Via della Dataria back into the city center at Via della Pilotta. Keep going north.

THE QUIRINALE TO VIA VENETO

THE QUIRINALE TO VIA VENETO   APPROX 1.8 MILES (2.9 KM)
TIME: APPROX 8.5 HOURS   METRO START: BARBERINI, LINE A

Map labels:
- Quattro Fontane
- San Carlo alle Quattro Fontane
- Sant'Andrea al Quirinale
- GIARDINO DEL QUIRINALE
- Piazza del Quirinale
- Scuderie del Quirinale
- DATARIA
- Fontana di Trevi
- PIAZZA DI TREVI
- VIA NAZIONALE
- VIA DEL QUIRINALE
- MONTE QUIRINALE
- VIA XXIV MAGGIO
- LARGO MAGNANAPOLI
- VIA DELLA PILOTTA
- VIA DELLA DATARIA
- VIA DELL'UMILTA
- VIA IN ARCIONE
- FONTANE

200 meters
200 yards
0
0

Quattro Fontane

1 Four small fountains, each of a reclining deity, mark the intersection of two roads and date from Pope Sixtus V's replanning of Rome in the late 16th century. This is the highest point of the Quirinale with stunning views in all four directions—of the **Palazzo del Quirinale, Santa Maria Maggiore, Trinità dei Monti,** and monumental **Porta Pia,** all but the latter marked by an obelisk.

Via delle Quattro Fontane (at Via del Quirinale) • Metro: Barberini, Line A • Bus: 71, 117

SAVVY **TRAVELER**

One of the Palazzo del Quirinale's most magnificent rooms is the Cappella Paolina (Pauline Chapel), designed by Carlo Maderno for Pope Paul V. On Sundays, excluding July through September, midday concerts of classical or Italian folk music are held here.

San Carlo alle Quattro Fontane

2 Despite being Francesco Borromini's first independent work (commissioned in 1634 but not completed until 1646), this church is a baroque jewel, affectionately known by the diminutive, "San Carlino." Making the most of a tiny space, Borromini's mathematical genius can be seen in the oval plan and architectural details: the shells and flowers that transform the niches and apses; the capitals, alternately inverted to vary the regularly spaced columns; and the ornate stucco on the dome. The aedicules were never destined to contain statues; instead, they sculpt the architectural space and emphasize the sweeping curves of the interior. Don't miss the tranquil cloister attached to the church—another gem full of inventive shapes.

Via delle Quattro Fontane 23 • 06 488 3261 • Metro: Barberini, Line A • Bus: 71, 117

Sant'Andrea al Quirinale

3 Completed in 1670, Sant'Andrea was the favorite building of the prolific architect Gian Lorenzo Bernini and an answer to his rival Borromini's earlier San Carlino. Sant'Andrea's patrons, the wealthy Jesuits, spared no expense for a church that served the richest and most powerful of Rome's elite—the cardinals who lived on the Quirinale close to the pope. Bernini used every technique in his power—fabulous veined marbles, stuccoed putti dangling from pediments, and dramatic stained-glass lighting—to make entry into the church a dazzling and sensory religious experience. The altarpiece shows the crucified Sant'Andrea (St. Andrew) himself.

Via del Quirinale 29 • 06 474 4801 • Metro: Barberini, Line A • Bus: 40, 64, 70, 170

Piazza del Quirinale

4 The piazza focuses on a great **obelisk,** flanked by two marble, fourth-century **Roman statues of Castor and Pollux,** the warrior sons of Jupiter, from the nearby Baths of Constantine. The obelisk is one of five that were carved by the Romans to imitate ancient Egyptian originals. With its partner on the Esquilino (Esquiline Hill), it once stood at the entrance to the Mausoleum of Augustus. Behind this monumental group, on the crest of the Quirinale, stands the **Palazzo del Quirinale** (*www.quirinale.it,* *06 46991, open Sun., June–Sept.*), its present design dating from the 1730s. Formerly the official residence of the kings of Italy, and since 1946 of the presidents of the republic, the palazzo remains Rome's most important political stronghold.

Statues line the balustrade that hugs the Piazza del Quirinale. Steps lead directly from the street to the northern end of the square and its namesake palazzo.

Via XXIV Maggio • Metro: Barberini, Line A • Bus: 40, 64, 70, 170

Scuderie del Quirinale

5 The Scuderie were the papal stables, completed in 1732, and restored and internally redesigned for the Jubilee Year 2000. The building is now one of Rome's leading cultural venues, with exhibitions held on the spacious second and third floors.

Via XXIV Maggio 16 • www.scuderiequirinale.it • 06 3996 7500 • €€€ • Metro: Barberini, Line A • Bus: 40, 64, 70, 170

Fontana di Trevi

6 Tucked between narrow streets, the fantastic and grand Trevi Fountain, commissioned by Pope Clement XII in 1732, fits gloriously with the Eternal City. Its water gushes from the Aqua Virgo (Virgin Aqueduct), an important ancient aqueduct named for the purity of its water. **Bas-reliefs** illustrate the legend that the Romans discovered the aqueduct's rural source with the help of a young girl, rather than by their usual scientific means. The central figure, the **Ocean,** is flanked by **statues of Abundance** and **Good Health.** The water was reputedly so sweet that whoever drank it would return to Rome. This may have given rise to the modern legend that whoever throws a coin (backward over their left shoulder) into the fountain will return to the city. The relatively unknown Niccolò Salvi forfeited his life designing the fountain—he died of complications after spending too much time in damp underground passages.

Via delle Muratte • www.trevifountain.net • Metro: Barberini, Line A • Bus: 52, 61, 62, 63, 95, 116

GOOD **EATS**

■ **IL GELATO DI SAN CRISPINO**
Homemade ice cream beckons conveniently near the Fontana di Trevi. **Via Panetteria 42, 06 679 3924, €**

■ **GIOIA MIA PISCIAPIANO**
This cozy trattoria near Piazza Barberini serves classic Roman pasta dishes like carbonara and *amatriciana,* and pizzas from a wood-fired oven. Closed on Sundays. **Via degli Avignonesi 34, 06 488 2784, €€€**

■ **RISTORANTE NINO**
Established in the 1930s, this wood-paneled restaurant near the Spanish Steps is renowned for high-quality Tuscan fare. **Via Borgognona 11, 06 679 5676, €€€€**

Palazzo Barberini

7 See pp. 94–95.

Via delle Quattro Fontane 13 • www.galleriaborghese .it • 06 32810 • €€ • Closed Mon., Jan. 1, and Dec. 25 • Metro: Barberini, Line A • Bus: 52, 61, 95, 116, 492, 590

Santa Maria della Concezione dei Cappuccini

8 The artistic attractions of this church include Guido Reni's **"The Archangel St. Michael,"** showing the archangel trampling the Devil, and Caravaggio's **"St. Francis in Prayer,"** which depicts the saint contemplating a skull. Nowadays perhaps more visitors are drawn by the skulls and skeletons in the crypt's

The clothed skeletons of eight friars watch over part of the crypt in Santa Maria della Concezione.

ossuary, in which the **bones of 4,000 friars** are arranged in a floor-to-ceiling mosaic. Created between 1631 and 1870, this crypt is the ultimate expression of the cult of the dead, and the viewer is reminded of this by a panel that reads: "What you are now, we were; what we are now, you shall be."

Via Veneto 27 • www.cappucciniviaveneto.it • 06 487 1185 • Donation: minimum €
• Metro: Barberini, Line A • Bus: 52, 53, 63, 80, 95, 116

Via Veneto

9 During the 1960s, the Via Veneto (full name Via Vittorio Veneto), made famous in Federico Fellini's film *La Dolce Vita* (the sweet life), epitomized Italian style—it was the haunt of movie stars and other glamorous celebrities. The Via Veneto's great palazzi now house embassies and goverment offices, and the glitterati have long gone, but visitors can sip a drink (though overpriced) at one of the pavement cafés and picture the past glories of this historic street.

Between Porta Pinciana and Piazza Barberini • Metro: Barberini, Line A • Bus: 52, 53, 63, 80, 95, 116

Palazzo Barberini

This magnificent baroque palace contains architectural and artistic jewels.

The gallery is a must for lovers of antique, Renaissance, and baroque art.

Having shot to power with the election of Maffeo Barberini to the papacy in 1624, the Barberini family created one of Rome's most imposing palaces between 1625 and 1633. They chose the great architect Carlo Maderno to design the building. But he was by then an old man, and the palace is now remembered more for his two assistants, who completed the project after his death: Bernini and Borromini. Since 1949, the palace has housed the treasures of Italy's Galleria Nazionale d'Arte Antica (National Gallery of Historic Art).

THE QUIRINALE TO VIA VENETO

■ SALONE DI PIETRO DA CORTONA

Designed by Bernini, the *salone* was the biggest waiting room in Rome and clearly intended to impress, if not stupefy, its visitors. Pietro da Cortona decorated the ceiling between 1632 and 1639 with a stunning illusionistic fresco, **"The Triumph of Divine Providence and Barberini Power."** To promote the recent election of Maffeo Barberini as Pope Urban VIII, Pietro created a piece of propaganda in the most extravagant baroque style. The ceiling seems to open up to the sky, where swirling figures hold emblems of the papacy—St. Peter's keys and a tiara—around the three Barberini bees.

■ SPIRAL STAIRCASE

Possibly the most beautiful architectural element of the palace is Borromini's aesthetically simple but structurally complex **oval staircase**, which consists of a single helix. Don't miss Bernini's **bust of Urban VIII.**

■ RAPHAEL'S "LA FORNARINA"

In Room 1, this mysterious painting was one of the last by the amorous Raphael before his early death in 1520.

IN **THE KNOW**

Rooms on the ground floor devoted to 12th- to 15th-century painting were once occupied by Urban VIII's nephew, Antonio Barberini, whom the pope made a cardinal.

The sitter is said to represent his lover, La Fornarina, the daughter of a baker (*fornaio*) from Trastevere. She sits in an obscured landscape, lit only by the moon, and is scantily dressed. Her left hand seems to conceal what the spice red cloth fails to, and her armband is inscribed with the artist's name.

■ CARAVAGGIO'S DARK REALISM

Room 8 houses Caravaggio's **"Judith and Holofernes"** (ca 1599), a violent and realistic painting that predates the artist's first major public commission. Here, a sanctified killing (the moment at which Judith saved the Jews) has been turned into a brutal murder with an undeniably sexual twist, if only because the model for Judith was one of Rome's most famous prostitutes. **"Narcissus"** is a more tranquil painting inspired by the myth about the dangers of vanity.

Galleria Nazionale d'Arte Antica di Palazzo Barberini • Via delle Quattro Fontane 13 • www.galleriaborghese.it • 06 32810 • €€ • Closed Mon., Jan. 1, and Dec. 25 • Metro: Barberini, Line A • Bus: 52, 61, 95, 116, 492, 590

Fountains & Aqueducts

The extensive aqueduct system constructed by the Romans carried water from rural sources up to 56 miles (90 km) away to the city's public baths, fountains, and latrines, and to the houses of the rich and powerful. Centuries later, successive popes beautified Rome and increased their prestige by having the ancient aqueducts reconnected and by funding ornate new fountains to provide a constant supply of clean water for public use.

Bernini's Fontana del Tritone is named for a magnificent sea monster, half man, half fish (above). The Fontana di Nettuno (right), named for the sea god Neptune, in Piazza Navona dates from 1574.

A Roman official named Appius Claudius Caecus, also the initiator of the Via Appia, commissioned the first aqueduct in 312 B.C. At the height of the Roman empire, a total of 11 of these magnificent structures converged on the capital. Later, through neglect and destruction in sieges, the water supply dwindled, leaving one aqueduct—the Aqua Virgo—functioning. The great aqueducts crumbled for almost a millennium, until the mid-15th century when Pope Nicholas V started renovating the Aqua Virgo, a conduit for water from northeast of Rome.

Fountains Galore

Restored aqueducts meant a relative abundance of water, and people needed access to that water—via public fountains. Among the oldest is the octagonal one in the **Piazza di Santa Maria in Trastevere,** created by architect Donato Bramante in the 1470s and still a focal point of its neighborhood. Over time, the fountains became more and more elaborate. In the 17th century, sculptor Gian Lorenzo Bernini created or contributed to many of the best loved,

THE QUIRINALE TO VIA VENETO

including the **Fontana dei Quattro Fiumi** and **Fontana del Moro** in Piazza Navona (see p. 123), and the **Fontana del Tritone** in Piazza Barberini.

Some were created by recycling ancient bits and pieces. In Via Giulia, the **Fontana del Mascherone** (Fountain of the Grotesque Mask), dating to 1626, comprises a marble face spurting water into a stone basin, both Roman in origin.

Local Themes

The tradition continued. In 1927, architect Pietro Lombardi designed a series of fountains with local themes. The triangular **Fontana degli Arti** in Via Margutta, known for its art galleries, is shaped like two easels. The petite but beautiful **Fontanella delle Tiare** near the Vatican is based on papal headwear.

(see p. 123)

AQUEDUCT **SITES**

Arch of Drusus From the early third century A.D., this arch once formed part of a larger aqueduct that Caracalla built to supply his baths half a mile (0.8 km) to the west. **Via di Porta San Sebastiano**

Parco degli Acquedotti This public park in Rome's eastern periphery is named for the seven historic aqueducts whose remains are preserved in situ. **Via Lemonaia**

Porta Maggiore This rugged arch was part of a double aqueduct built in the east of the city under Emperor Claudius in A.D. 52. **Piazzale Labricano**

THE QUIRINALE TO VIA VENETO

Food & Fashion Shops

While Rome hasn't escaped the pressures of globalization—many mass-market international brands have entered key locations—the city has nevertheless maintained its edge as one of the most fascinating and satisfying shopping destinations in Europe, especially if your vices are food and fashion.

■ GOURMET HEAVEN

With 11 locations around the Italian capital, **Castroni** is the dominant purveyor of gourmet food in Rome. Visitors are most likely to come across branches in the Quirinale neighborhood *(Via Nazionale 71)* and on the Vatican side of Rome *(Via Cola di Rienzo 196)*. Castroni combines top-notch Italian foods, hundreds of tea and coffee blends, and rare international delicacies and ingredients. A few blocks south from the splendid Santa Maria Maggiore church on the Esquilino, **Panella** *(Via Merulana 54)* was born as an upscale bakery and evolved into a gourmet store that offers the fanciest bread and pastry in town as well a rich assortment of everything and anything that delights the palate. Farther south, **Volpetti** *(Via Marmorata 47)* has built its reputation as the most famous gourmet destination of the Testaccio

neighborhood. A self-declared temple of old-fashioned flavors, this family-run business gladly welcomes guests for lunch. **Trimani** *(Via Goito 20)*, east of Via XX Settembre, has supplied Romans with the finest wines and spirits, both Italian and international, since 1821. With 4,500 labels in stock, only few dare to question its primacy in the capital. Those wanting to try before they buy should head to the **Trimani Wine Bar** *(Via Cernaia 37)* right around the corner.

■ LUXURY & ULTRA-BOUTIQUE

The city's main luxury shopping area extends from Piazza di Spagna to Via del Corso and Largo C. Goldoni. Take in Via dei Condotti, home to **Valentino** *(No. 15)* and two **Bulgari** stores *(Nos. 10 and 61–63)*, and the parallel Via Borgognona. At Largo C. Goldoni, historic **Palazzo Fendi** reigns supreme, and a few steps to the left, elegant

Immaculate shirts are lined up in perfect formation in one of Rome's many independent shops.

Piazza San Lorenzo in Lucina offers a handful of Italian fashion legends and some top international labels, such as **Louis Vuitton** *(No. 36)*. Finally, **Via del Babuino,** between Piazza di Spagna and Piazza del Popolo, features many luxury shops of Italian, French, British, and Spanish origin. In the historic center just west of Piazza Navona, head to **Via del Governo Vecchio**—its unassuming boutiques sell exclusively sourced styles and are much frequented by local well-to-do ladies. While in the historic center, look out for branches of **Gente,** the high-end multibrand concept store.

■ FASHION AT GREAT PRICES

Rome is one of Italy's garment production hubs, with homegrown brands that invest in quality and trendiness rather than in brand notoriety. This makes them ideal for the value-conscious fashionista. You'll find a number of mid-premium brands with strong Roman roots—such as **LIST** womens' store and men's outfitters **David Mayer Naman**—on Via Frattina, off Via del Corso, on Via Cola di Rienzo, near the Vatican, and on Via Nazionale, running between Piazza Venezia and Piazza della Repubblica.

Piazza di Spagna to Villa Borghese

Wedged between the Tiber and the sprawling Villa Borghese, the northern part of central Rome is an eclectic neighborhood that mixes ancient monuments and churches with chic boutiques and cafés. In imperial times this was the Campo Marzio (Field of Mars), an open area bisected by the main road between Rome and the rest of continental Europe. The area's importance waned in the Middle Ages but revived in the Renaissance, and later the district evolved into a foreign quarter, catering to merchants, diplomats, and a bounty of writers and artists hoping that Rome would prove their muse. From early times, the heights above the plain (now the Villa Borghese park and Pincio gardens) were the haunt of the rich and powerful—Roman aristocrats, medieval popes, and Renaissance nobles who created fabulous villas and gardens.

◐ **As ever, the scene is colorful on the Spanish Steps, leading from Piazza di Spagna to the church of Santissima Trinità dei Monti.**

6 The Pincio (see p. 106)
Take in the view from a hilltop where nobles and popes once cavorted. Walk the Viale dell'Obelisco into the main part of the Villa Borghese park, then head north.

7 Villa Giulia (see p. 106–107) Etruscan treasures are the forte of this former papal residence. Viale delle Belle Arti leads into the heart of the Villa Borghese park.

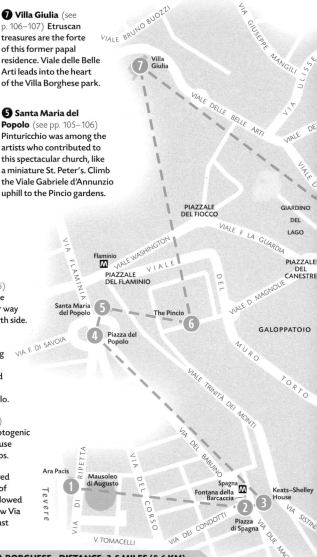

5 Santa Maria del Popolo (see pp. 105–106) Pinturicchio was among the artists who contributed to this spectacular church, like a miniature St. Peter's. Climb the Viale Gabriele d'Annunzio uphill to the Pincio gardens.

4 Piazza del Popolo (see p. 105)
The oval plaza is flanked by ornate statuary and churches. Make your way to the church on the square's north side.

3 Keats–Shelley House (see p. 105) Pay homage to the guiding lights of the Romantic era in the house where John Keats lived and died. Follow the Via del Babuino northwest to the Piazza del Popolo.

2 Piazza di Spagna (see p. 104)
The Spanish Steps crown this photogenic plaza. Head for the four-story house at the bottom of the Spanish Steps.

1 Ara Pacis (see p. 104) Restored to its ancient splendor, the Altar of Peace marks the stability that followed Rome's imperial conquests. Follow Via Tomacelli and Via dei Condotti east toward the Spanish Steps.

**PIAZZA DI SPAGNA TO VILLA BORGHESE   DISTANCE: 3.5 MILES (5.6 KM)
TIME: APPROX. 8 HOURS   METRO START: SPAGNA, LINE A**

PIAZZA DI SPAGNA TO VILLA BORGHESE

Piazza di Spagna to Villa Borghese

The Spanish Steps and shady alleys of the Villa Borghese park are among the highlights in a walk that takes in a sacrificial altar, churches, and fascinating museums.

GIARDINO
ZOOLOGICO

GIARDINO ZOOLOGICO

PIAZZALE
DEL
GIARDINO
ZOOLOGICO

PARCO
DEI
DAINI

VIALE GIULIA

VIALE PIETRO CANONICA

VIALE DELL'UCCELLIERA

VIALE DEI CAVALLI MARINI

Galleria
Borghese

9

BORGHESE

8

PIAZZA DI
SIENA

Villa
Borghese

VIALE S PAOLO D BRASILE

VIALE DEL MUSEO

PIAZZA
BRASILE

VIA DI PORTA PINCIANA

VIA FRANCESCO CRISPI

| 0 | 400 meters |
| 0 | 400 yards |

9 **Galleria Borghese** (see pp. 108–109) **One of Europe's top art museums—housed in the actual villa from which the Villa Borghese park gets its name—showcases Renaissance and baroque masters.**

8 **Villa Borghese** (see p. 107) Rome's great green escape, the rambling park provides plenty of scope for rest, relaxation, or recreation. Meander to the park's northeastern corner.

The chief glory of the Ara Pacis is the set of exquisitely carved friezes that adorn the exterior. They are all rendered in the finest Carrara marble.

Ara Pacis

1 The Pax Romana is the theme of this ancient monument on the banks of the Tiber. Reconstructed in the 1930s from remnants scattered across scores of museums, the Ara Pacis (Altar of Peace) was commissioned by the Roman senate as a tribute to Emperor Augustus and the peace that followed his imperial expansion. The rectangular structure is now enclosed within a museum designed by American architect Richard Meier and opened in 2006. The monument is covered in intricate carvings, including renderings of Augustus and his family, a scene that may have represented the dedication of the Ara Pacis in 13 B.C. Across the street is the crumbling Mausoleum of Augustus, no longer open to visitors and badly in need of restoration.

Lungotevere in Augusta • http://en.arapacis.it • 06 06 08 • €€€ • Closed Mon. • Metro: Spagna, Flaminio, Line A

Piazza di Spagna

2 Named for the Spanish Embassy that once overlooked the square, the Piazza di Spagna has been the coolest place to hang out in Rome for nearly 300 years. The neighborhood has long attracted foreigners—Lord Byron, Keats, Shelley, Goethe, Ibsen, Oscar Wilde, James Joyce, and Hans Christian Andersen are among the artistic hipsters who frequented the local inns and cafés. The **Spanish Steps** were added in the 1720s to connect the square with **Santissima Trinità dei Monti,** the Renaissance church on the hilltop above. **La Barcaccia,** the boat-shaped fountain at the base of the Spanish Steps, predates the stairway by a hundred years. The area's chic boutiques are a recent addition.

Between Via dei Condotti and Via della Croce • Metro: Spagna, Line A

Keats–Shelley House

3 Perched on the south side of the Spanish Steps, the building is a holy grail of the early 19th-century English Romantic movement. Poet John Keats moved here in 1820 and died, aged 25, from tuberculosis the following year. Percy Bysshe Shelley lived nearby. He perished in 1822 when he drowned off the Italian coast. Memories of them linger on, as do those of the other Romantics that round out the collection of this marvelous small museum. Exhibits include Keats's death mask and an original manuscript by Mary Shelley, wife of the poet and author of *Frankenstein*.

Piazza di Spagna 26 • www.keats-shelley-house.org • 06 678 4235 • €€ • Closed Sun. • Metro: Spagna, Line A

Piazza del Popolo

4 Once the spot where religious heretics were executed, the Piazza del Popolo is now the "people's square" and a venue for mass political gatherings. From here a Roman road called the Via Flaminia began its journey north up the Italian Peninsula. On the square's southern side, baroque twin churches—**Santa Maria dei Miracoli** and **Santa Maria in Montesanto**—flank the Via del Corso. The whitewashed **Porta del Popolo** on the northern side was Rome's primary gateway through much of the Middle Ages and beyond. Architect Giuseppe Valadier conceived the current square in the early 19th century, including ramps and steps that ascend the **Pincio** and an Egyptian **obelisk** that once graced the Circo Massimo.

Between Via del Corso and Via Flaminia • Metro: Flaminio, Line A

Santa Maria del Popolo

5 Raphael, Caravaggio, and Bramante were among the Italian masters who contributed to this lavish church on the north side of the Piazza del Popolo. According to legend, the original church on the site was created to vanquish the ghost of the long-dead Roman emperor Nero, who was buried nearby. It was replaced by the current Renaissance structure, commissioned in 1472 by Pope Sixtus IV della Rovere. Among several frescoes by Pinturicchio, don't miss a delightful **"Adoration of the Christ Child"** above the altar in the Della Rovere Chapel. Raphael designed the ornate **Chigi Chapel** for the wealthy banker Agostino Chigi. A pair of Caravaggio masterpieces—**"The Conversion of St. Paul on the Road to Damascus"** and **"The Crucifixion of St. Peter"**—hang in the Cerasi Chapel.

Piazza del Popolo 12 • www.santamariadelpopolo.it • 06 361 0836 • Metro: Flaminio, Line A

The Pincio

6 The lofty green space above the Piazza del Popolo is the Pincio garden, the western sector of the extensive Villa Borghese gardens, but in many respects its own little world replete with busts

of notable Italians, an unusual water clock, and the **San Carlino marionette theater** (*Viale dei Bambini, Villa Borghese, 06 6992 2117*). The symmetry between square and garden is not accidental: Giuseppe Valadier designed both during the French occupation of Rome under Napoleon. The **Piazza Napoleone** is an excellent perch to view the Popolo neighborhood directly below and St. Peter's in the distance.

W side of the Villa Borghese • Metro: Flaminio, Line A

A biblical theme inspired this fountain in the Pincio—Moses' mother setting her baby son afloat in his bullrush basket.

Villa Giulia

7 Built as a country palace for Pope Julius III in the 1550s, the ornate Renaissance villa now houses the **Museo Nazionale Etrusco,** Italy's premier showcase of regional art and artifacts predating the Roman Empire. Among its many treasures are the Etruscan **Sarcofago**

degli Sposi (Sarcophagus of the Spouses), an incredibly lifelike terra-cotta rendering of a married couple reclining on a banquet sofa, from the sixth century B.C. Set in the northwest corner of the Villa Borghese, the building reflects the extravagant lifestyle of Renaissance popes, in particular a two-story **nymphaeum** (water grotto) in the garden where Julius entertained guests in summer.

Piazzale di Villa Giulia 9, Villa Borghese • 06.322.6571 • €€€
• Closed Mon. • Metro: Flaminio, Line A

Villa Borghese

8 Cardinal Scipione Borghese, who created the villa and its surrounding gardens, amassed a substantial fortune in the early 17th century via family connections and a devious nature that would have put Machiavelli to shame. The villa now houses the **Galleria Borghese** (see pp. 108–109), while the gardens have become Rome's most popular park. Stroll along gravel pathways shaded by umbrella pines—perfect on a hot day—and admire statues and classical-style ornamental temples. At the center is the **Giardino del Lago** (Garden of the Lake), with its boating lake. Don't miss the delightful art nouveau **Fontana dei Fauni** (Fountain of the Fauns). At the north end of the park, the **Galleria Nazionale d'Arte Moderna** has a good display of 19th- and 20th-century art.

Between Via Flaminia (to the west) and Via Pinciana (to the east) • Metro: Flaminio, Spagna, Line A

Galleria Borghese

9 See pp. 108–109.

Piazzale del Museo Borghese 5 • www.galleriaborghese.it • 06 841 3979
• €€€ • Closed Mon. • Metro: Flaminio, Spagna, Barberini, Line A

GOOD **EATS**

■ **ANTICO CAFFÈ GRECO**
Casanova, Byron, and Wagner were habitués of this atmospheric café near the Spanish Steps. Coffee, tea, and hot chocolate are specialties. **Via dei Condotti 84, 06 679 1700, €**

■ **CAFFÈ CANOVA-TADOLINI**
A hip hangout between Spagna and Popolo doubles as a museum dedicated to sculptors Antonio Canova and Adamo Tadolini. Enjoy snacks, pasta dishes, and scrumptious desserts. **Via del Babuino 150a, 06 3211 0702, €€€**

■ **CASINA VALADIER**
The menu at this upscale eatery in the Villa Borghese offers a modern take on pasta and meat dishes. But the stars are the view and romantic ambience. **Piazza Bucarest, Villa Borghese, 06 6992 2090, €€€€**

PIAZZA DI SPAGNA TO VILLA BORGHESE

Galleria Borghese

Described as an "Elysium of Delight" by English tourist John Evelyn in 1644, the world's finest private collection of art never fails to enchant visitors.

Correggio's "Danäe" shows the beautiful princess—one of Jupiter's many lovers—with Cupid.

The Villa Borghese, housing the Galleria Borghese, originated as a temple to pleasure, a place to show off the art that belonged to Cardinal Scipione Borghese (1577–1633), a nephew of Pope Paul V. He would bring guests through the landscaped gardens and wow them with lavish banquets, entertainments, and his stunning collection. Although Napoleon later carried off many of the prized ancient sculptures to the Louvre in Paris, the core Renaissance collection and the baroque pieces that Scipione commissioned for the villa are still in place.

◼ OLD MASTERS

Scipione Borghese collected all the greats. Upstairs on the first floor are paintings by Renaissance masters, including Titian's **"Sacred and Profane Love,"** Raphael's **"Deposition,"** and Lucas Cranach's **"Venus and Cupid with a Honeycomb."** Also not to be missed are two works by Piero della Francesca, the **"Flagellation,"** a masterly study in perspective, and the hypnotic **"Senigallia Madonna."**

◼ BERNINI MASTERPIECES

Occupying pride of place on the ground floor are the real showstoppers of the collection: four sculptures by the cardinal's favorite living artist, Gian Lorenzo Bernini, that Scipione commissioned especially for the villa. **"Aeneas Escaping Troy"** is an early work, but **"Pluto and Proserpine," "Apollo and Daphne,"** and **"David"** (a self-portrait) represent the height of baroque brilliance. On the first floor, look out for two **marble busts of Scipione** flanking a **Bernini self-portrait.** And don't miss **"The Goat Amalthea With the Infant Jupiter and a Faun,"** which Bernini reputedly sculpted at the age of 13.

SAVVY **TRAVELER**

Make sure you reserve tickets in advance, and arrive on time; the gallery limits your visit. Don't go up to the main entrance— use the stairs at the back right-hand corner of the ticket office. These will take you to the picture galleries on the first floor, allowing you to avoid the majority of the crowd, who will start downstairs.

◼ CARAVAGGIO

Also on the ground floor is Caravaggio's **"David with the Head of Goliath."** Scipione supported the controversial artist, despite his tumultuous personal life. Caravaggio sent the work to his patron in 1610, four years after he had fled Rome after killing a man in a brawl—in the hope that Scipione would secure a papal pardon for him.

◼ PAULINE BONAPARTE

Another ground floor highlight is Antonio Canova's marble statue of Napoleon's sister Pauline, who was married to a Borghese descendant, Prince Camillo. Depicting her as a semi-naked Venus, it caused a scandal when unveiled in 1808. When asked how she could have posed in this way, she replied: "I had a fire to keep me warm."

PIAZZA DI SPAGNA TO VILLA BORGHESE

Piazzale del Museo Borghese 5 • www.galleriaborghese.it • 06 841 3979 • €€€ • Closed Mon.
• Metro: Flaminio, Spagna, Barberini, Line A

La Dolce Vita

All Italians have a reputation for enjoying the good life—*la dolce vita*—to the fullest. Surrounded by the glories of an ancient past, and by the finest Renaissance and baroque art and architecture, Romans especially have an exalted sense of aesthetic, which they carry over into savoring the pleasures of life. In the words of the late fashion designer Gianni Versace, "You decide what you are and what you want to express by the way you dress and the way you live."

Bar della Pace near Piazza Navona has long been a magnet for artists and glitterati (above). In *La Dolce Vita*, Swedish actress Anita Ekberg famously frolicked in the Fontana di Trevi with Marcello Mastroianni (right).

Romans on Parade

The Italian love of display is most manifest during the evening *passeggiata*, or stroll, from around 7 to 8 p.m. People dress up and step out with friends, partners, and families, to mingle, saunter, and look at each other. Though this is more of a ritual in provincial cities, Romans also flow out into the streets at this hour—part of the Via del Corso is pedestrianized in the evening for this purpose.

En route they will drop into a bar to watch the world go by while sipping an *aperitivo* such as prosecco or campari, always served with some tasty snack, perhaps olives or a tiny pizza. Elegant venues for this engaging pastime include **Canova** *(Piazza del Popolo)* and **Bar Farnese** *(Piazza Farnese 106)*. Trendier bohemian spots are the 18th-century, ivy-clad **Bar della Pace** *(Via della Pace 3–7)* and nearby **Bar del Fico** *(Piazza del Fico 26)*.

Romans are equally likely to get together for a post-dinner ice cream. To join in the fun, head to **Gelateria del Teatro** in a cobbled alley *(Via di San Simone 70)*, serving up flavorsome, organic

PIAZZA DI SPAGNA TO VILLA BORGHESE

treats such as chocolate with red wine. **Claudio Torcè** (*Viale Aventino 59*) and **Gelateria dei Gracchi** (*Via dei Gracchi 272*) also rank high on the ice-cream gourmet's hit list. So much a part of Roman life is the gelato experience that it's quite usual to see besuited businessmen buzzing around with a tub of pistacchio or *stracciatella* in hand.

Food, Family, and Friends

Mealtimes are, of course, a prime source of social and gastronomic delight. Lunch requires at least two courses; dinner, at around 9 p.m., will be three or more. Discover the secret of family-run restaurants beloved by Romans, such as **Da Enzo** (*Via dei Vascellari 29*), dropping by **Caffè Ciampini** (*Piazza Trinità dei Monti*) for a dessert with a view.

Federico Fellini's 1960 landmark film, *La Dolce Vita,* ensured that the phrase was assimilated into English to denote a love of life's pleasures and the Italian skill in elevating this to an art form. Set in a decadent contemporary Rome, the film expresses Fellini's own love affair with the capital, which started with his arrival as a poor and hungry 18-year-old. He was captivated by sights and smells such as the "resplendent cheese stores, the smell of warm bread . . . the pastry shops." Fellini's fascination with Rome also encompassed the harsh reality of its street life and the amorality of its jet set.

PIAZZA DI SPAGNA TO VILLA BORGHESE

Mosaics

Rome's medieval churches reveal stunning works of mosaic—shimmering gold-and-glass scenes of saints and biblical stories that come alive in undulating ripples of color. All too often overshadowed by the city's ancient, Renaissance, and baroque art, these gems from the Middle Ages are well worth searching out.

PIAZZA DI SPAGNA TO VILLA BORGHESE

■ SANTA MARIA DEL POPOLO
An unusual example of a High Renaissance mosaic lines the dome of Santa Maria del Popolo's (see pp. 105–106) **Chigi Chapel.** Raphael designed both the mosaic and the chapel for his friend, banker Agostino Chigi. The mosaic depicts the creation of the world and the planets.

Piazza del Popolo 12 • 06 361 0836

■ SAN CLEMENTE
The 12th-century apse of San Clemente (see pp. 63–64) is a peculiar break from contemporary mosaic tradition. Rather than showing Christ with various saints, the work illustrates curving tendrils that hide tiny men, women, and animals. Art historians theorize that the apse mosaic is a copy of a mosaic from the fourth-century church whose remains lie beneath the 12th-century church.

Via di San Giovanni in Laterano 108 • 06 774 0021

■ SANTA MARIA MAGGIORE
The basilica (see p. 78) crowns the Esquilino (Esquiline Hill). The mosaics above the nave colonnade are a series of Old Testament scenes. Dating from the fifth century, they owe their animated style to ancient Roman artwork. Note the attention to narrative and architectural detail—absent from the 13th-century mosaics in the apse.

Piazza Santa Maria Maggiore • 06 6988 6800

■ SANTA PRASSEDE
Located just off Piazza Santa Maria Maggiore, Santa Prassede (see p. 78) boasts the splendid ninth-century **St. Zeno Chapel,** covered in tiny glass tiles from floor to ceiling. Four angels and a medallion of Christ cover the ceiling, while floral patterns and pictures of saints embellish the walls. The apse in the main church is another mosaic masterpiece.

Via di Santa Prassede 9a • 06 488 2456

Doves share the cross with Christ in the beautiful apse mosaic in San Clemente.

■ SANTA MARIA IN TRASTEVERE

In the heart of Trastevere, the Church of Santa Maria in Trastevere (see p. 152) preserves 12th-century mosaics both inside and out. On the facade, the Virgin Mary sits enthroned with the infant Christ. The pair are flanked by attendants bearing gifts. Inside, the apse is clad in one of Rome's finest mosaic works. Mary, Christ, and saints are dressed in shimmering royal garments. Below them are mosaics depicting the life of the Virgin. Created by Roman artist Pietro Cavallini in the late 13th century, these are laid in a style that rejects the stiffness of the Middle Ages and embraces a naturalism and plasticity that foreshadows the Renaissance.

Piazza Santa Maria in Trastevere • 06 581 9443

■ SANTA CECILIA IN TRASTEVERE

Also in Trastevere, the front portico of Santa Cecilia (see pp. 150–151) is trimmed with a delicate mosaic frieze showing garlands, portraits, and birds. Inside the church, the ninth-century apse depicts a larger-than-life Christ floating on a dark blue background. To his left, St. Cecilia embraces Pope Paschal I.

Piazza Santa Cecilia 22 • 06 589 9289

Pantheon to Piazza Navona

The area stretching south and west from the Pantheon toward the Tiber River has been an integral part of Rome's fabric since ancient times. Leaders such as Julius Caesar, Pompey, Marcus Agrippa, and Augustus built temples, theaters, and bathing complexes here. During the Middle Ages, Rome's population adapted and transformed these antiquities, building a church inside the mighty Pantheon and using ancient structures as foundations for the church of Santa Maria sopra Minerva and the Piazza Navona, itself a prime example of baroque-era development. In the 16th century, the Palazzo Farnese became the command center of the Farnese family, while artisans and traders worked in and around Campo de' Fiori. The monument to King Vittorio Emanuele II has kept up the area's tradition of spectacular buildings.

❍ **Many Renaissance buildings remain in this part of Rome—such as these on Vicolo della Moretta, just off Via Giulia.**

PANTHEON TO PIAZZA NAVONA

Pantheon to Piazza Navona

Walk from Rome's best preserved ancient building to some of its most picturesque squares, streets, and churches.

PANTHEON TO PIAZZA NAVONA

⑩ **Piazza Navona** (see p. 123)
As you enter Rome's largest and most charming square, the Fontana del Moro is in front of you with the Fontana dei Quattro Fiumi beyond.

⑨ **Via Giulia** (see p. 123)
The 16th-century avenue is home to palaces and churches. Turn right into Vicolo della Moretta, go through Piazza della Chiesa Nuova into Via della Chiesa Nuova, then right on Via del Governo Vecchio until you reach Piazza Navona.

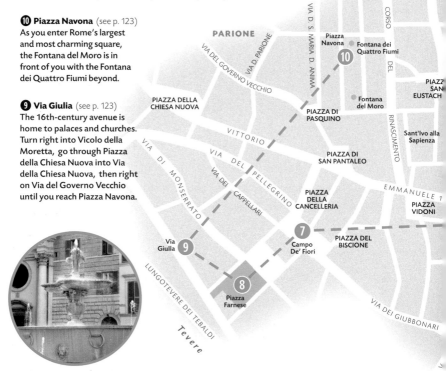

⑧ **Piazza Farnese**
(see p. 122) The elegant square is dominated by the luxurious Palazzo Farnese, a noble palace completed by Michelangelo. The Via Giulia is directly behind the palace.

⑦ **Campo de' Fiori** (see p. 121) Simple Renaissance buildings encircle the *campo*, a marketplace by day, a destination for revelry by night. Take Via de' Balluari one block southwest.

⑥ **Largo di Torre Argentina** (see p. 121) Named for its medieval tower, Largo di Torre Argentina is home to four Roman temples and hundreds of cats. From Via Arenula, turn right and follow Via dei Giubbonari west.

**PANTHEON TO PIAZZA NAVONA   DISTANCE: 2.4 MILES (3.9 KM)
TIME: APPROX. 7 HOURS   BUS START: 46, 64, 70, 116 • TRAM: 8**

① Pantheon (see pp. 124–125) One of the most intact ancient buildings, the hulking Pantheon was a feat of engineering. Walk one block south on Piazza della Rotonda to the adjacent square, where a white facade gives way to Rome's only Gothic church.

② Santa Maria sopra Minerva (see p. 118) Intersecting vertical vaults rise above the church's funeral monuments and chapels. Leave through the rear door to the left of the main altar, and head east through Piazza del Collegio Romano to Via del Corso.

③ Palazzo Doria Pamphili (see p. 119) Occupying several city blocks, the palazzo is still inhabited by the noble family that gives the building its name. Follow the palazzo's facade south along the Via del Corso.

④ Piazza Venezia (see p. 120) The monument that celebrates Italy's unification dwarfs the surrounding buildings, even a large Renaissance palace nearby. Follow Via del Plebiscito two blocks west.

⑤ Il Gesù (see pp. 120–121) The Jesuit order's main church is a baroque treasure. Cross the piazza, and take Corso Vittorio Emanuele II three blocks west.

Fontana e Obelisco

PIAZZA DELLA ROTONDA

VIA DEL SEMINARIO

PIAZZA DI SANT'IGNAZIO

Pantheon

V. D. SANTIGNAZIO

VIA DEL CORSO

Santa Maria sopra Minerva

PIAZZA DELLA MINERVA

PIAZZA DEL COLLEGIO ROMANO

Palazzo Doria Pamphili

PIGNA

VIA D. TORRE ARGENTINA

V. C. BATTISTI

Largo di Torre Argentina

VIA DEL PLEBISCITO

Palazzo Venezia

Templi Repubblicani

PIAZZA DEL GESÙ

Il Gesù

Palazzetto di Venezia

VIA DELLE BOTTEGHE OSCURE

VIA SAN MARCO

Piazza Venezia

ENULA

0 ——————— 200 meters
0 ——————— 200 yards

PIAZZA D'ARACOELI

Pantheon

1 See pp. 124–125.

Piazza della Rotonda • 06 6830 0230 • Closed Jan. 1, May 1, and Dec. 25
• Bus: C3, 40, 46, 62, 63, 64, 70, 81, 87, 116, 119, 492, 628 • Tram: 8

DON'T **MISS**

The Church of San Luigi dei Francesi, between Piazza Navona and the Pantheon, houses three paintings by Caravaggio. The Contarelli Chapel, just to the left of the main altar, displays **"The Calling of St. Matthew," "The Evangelist Writes the Gospel,"** and **"The Martyrdom of St. Matthew."**

Santa Maria sopra Minerva

2 Don't let the nondescript white stone facade of Rome's only Gothic church deter you from entering. Once inside, the ornate interior of the tall central aisle, with thin marble column ribs supporting the vivid vaulted ceiling, gives you a feeling of lightness and grandeur. Thanks to the influence of the Dominican friars who built the church in the 13th century, it gained great prestige—four popes are buried here, along with a patron saint of Italy, St. Catherine of Siena. The side aisles are divided into chapels commissioned by nobles for private use.

In the right transept, the **Carafa Chapel** is one of Rome's greatest Renaissance treasures. Filippino Lippi painted the colorful fresco cycle on the ceiling and walls circa 1490. One scene shows St. Thomas Aquinas presenting Cardinal Oliviero Carafa to the Virgin Mary at **"The Annunciation,"** below a magnificent depiction of **"The Assumption of the Virgin."** The saint recurs in his signature black Dominican habit in **"The Triumph of St. Thomas Aquinas"** on the right-side wall. On the opposing wall rests the funeral monument of Pope Paul IV Carafa, the pontiff who notoriously established the Jewish Ghetto in 1555. To the right of the marble coffin in the main altar, which contains St. Catherine of Siena's remains, is Michelangelo's **"Christ the Redeemer,"** a marble statue of Jesus carrying the cross.

Piazza della Minerva 42 • 06 679 3926 • Bus: C3, 40, 46, 62, 63, 64, 70, 81, 87, 116, 119, 492, 628 • Tram: 8

PANTHEON TO PIAZZA NAVONA

The beautiful interior of the Palazzo Doria Pamphili presents a riot of decorative delights.

Palazzo Doria Pamphili

③ This 15th- to 17th-century building houses one of the city's largest private art collections. The walls of the Pamphili family's apartments, known as the *piano nobile* (first floor), are crowded with oil paintings by Renaissance and baroque masters such as Peter Paul Rubens, Titian, and Raphael. Highlights include Diego Velázquez's **"Portrait of Innocent X"** (Room X), which hangs beside Gian Lorenzo Bernini's sculpture of the same pontiff. Two paintings by Caravaggio—**"Penitent Magdalen"** and **"Rest on the Flight into Egypt"**—hang in Sala del 600, while his **"St. John the Baptist"** is in corridor 4. An audio guide (included in the admission price) is narrated by the current Prince Doria Pamphili, whose anecdotes enliven the collection's history.

Via del Corso 305 • www.dopart.it • 06 679 7323 • Closed Jan. 1, Easter Sun., and Dec. 25 • €€€ • Bus: 40, 46, 62, 63, 64, 70, 81, 85, 87, 95, 119, 175, 492, 628

Piazza Venezia

4 This busy traffic hub is home to the city's grandest building—the impressively ornate white marble **Monumento a Vittorio Emanuele II,** known as the Vittoriano. The 443-foot-wide (135 m) and 230-foot-high (70 m) monument was begun in 1885 to celebrate Italy's unification under King Victor Emanuel II, and it took five decades to complete. Its gleaming white embellishments borrow from ancient Roman iconography—chariots, winged goddesses, shields, and an equestrian statue all evoke the theme of victory. The tomb of the unknown soldier, flanked by Italian military personnel, is built into the facade, while a doorway on the southwestern side of the building gives access to the **Museo del Risorgimento** (*Piazza Venezia, 06 678 0664*), which recounts the history of Italy's unification movement. Also inside, take an elevator to the **Terrazza Panoramica** (*Piazza Venezia, 06 678 0905, €€*), a roof observation deck with wondrous panoramic views. On the western side of the square is the **Palazzo Venezia** (*Via del Plebiscito 118, 06 6999 4319, €, closed Jan. 1, May 1, and Dec. 25*), a Renaissance palace that hosts art exhibitions.

Piazza Venezia • Metro: Colosseo, Line B • Bus: 46, 60, 62, 63, 64, 119, 628, 715, 716, 780

GOOD **EATS**

■ **CUL DE SAC**
Set in a charming square south of Piazza Navone, this wine bar has outdoor seating and serves hot and cold plates and light meals, as well as an enormous selection of fine wines. **Piazza Pasquino 73, 06 6880 1094, €€**

■ **ROSCIOLI**
Not far from Campo de'Fiori, this elegant eatery serves some of the best carbonara and cured meats in town. **Via dei Giubbonari 21, 06 687 5287, €€€€€**

■ **VINO E CAMINO**
This casual restaurant near the Tiber offers a tasty selection of pasta, fish, meats, and vegetables. **Piazza dell'Oro 6, 06 6830 1332, €€€**

Il Gesù

5 Rome's first Jesuit church was consecrated in 1584; its opulent interior embodies the aesthetics and emotion of the Counter-Reformation spirit. The limestone facade gives way to a building shaped like a Latin cross, where frescoes in the dome and on the vaulted ceiling above the central aisle were painted in an energetic style by Baciccia, a pupil of Gian Lorenzo Bernini. Look up and you seem to peer directly into the heavenly realms. The Chapel of St. Ignatius in the left transept contains the relics of St. Ignatius Loyola, the founder of the Jesuit Order. Above the altar hangs Andrea Pozzo's painting of the saint's ascension. Next door, the rooms where St. Ignatius lived are open for two hours each day (Mon.–Sat. 4–6 p.m., Sun. 10 a.m.–12 noon).

Via degli Astalli 16 • www.chiesadelgesu.org • 06 69 7001 • Closed Sun. and daily 12:30 p.m.–4 p.m. • Bus: 46, 62, 63, 64, 70, 81, 84, 87, 492, 628

Largo di Torre Argentina

6 At the eastern end of Corso Vittorio Emanuele II are the sunken remains of four republican-era Roman temples from the third to second century B.C. The temples stood next to the later Pompey Theater complex, where the Roman general and dictator, Julius Caesar, was assassinated. Today, the columns, walls, and steps are home to a cat sanctuary, with many contented felines walking around the ancient stonework. Although you cannot walk among the ruins, you get a great view of them from street level.

Largo di Torre Argentina • www.romancats.com • Bus: H, 40 Express, 64 • Tram: 8

Campo de' Fiori

7 This elongated square, encircled by simple Renaissance buildings, hosts a fruit-and-vegetable market every morning. In the evening, however, the *campo* is a lively meeting point for the city's young people, who congregate in its outdoor cafés and bars. In the center of the square is a bronze **statue of Giordano Bruno,** a philosopher who was burned at the stake in 1600 during the Roman Inquisition.

Piazza Campo de' Fiori • Market open 8 a.m.–2 p.m.; closed Sun. • Bus: 40, 46, 62, 64, 70, 81, 116, 492, 628 • Tram: 8

Numerous well-fed cats are the beneficiaries of Pompey's ruined theater of 55 B.C. They can tread where humans are not allowed.

Piazza Farnese

8   The 16th-century **Palazzo Farnese** dominates this elegant square. Built for Cardinal Alessandro Farnese (who later became Pope Paul III), the palace shows off his family's power, wealth, and artistic tastes, and is arguably Rome's most beautiful Renaissance building. It was begun by architect Antonio da Sangallo and completed by Michelangelo, who introduced the heavy cornice at the top of the building—an innovation at the time. Today the palace is home to the French Embassy, so access is limited. From outside of the building, look into the ground-floor **"Fasti Farnesiani" hall** for a taste of the opulence within. At both ends of the square are **two granite-basin fountains** from the third-century Roman Terme di Caracalla, which were excavated by the Farnese family and added to the square in the 18th century.

Piazza Farnese • Bus: C3, 23, 46, 62, 63, 64, 70, 81, 87, 116, 280, 492, 628

Courtyards such as this one may be glimpsed along the elegant Via Giulia.

Via Giulia

9 One of Rome's most exclusive streets, the 0.6-mile (1 km) Via Giulia runs parallel to the banks of the Tiber. Pope Julius II had it carved out of the medieval maze of streets in 1508, as part of his project to redevelop the area. Running northwest from Ponte Sisto, Via Giulia is trimmed with noble Renaissance and baroque palaces and churches, including **San Eligio** *(No. 18),* which was probably designed by Raphael. The street's most prominent feature is the single **arch** at the southeastern end, which Michelangelo hoped would be completed to cross the river and connect the Palazzo Farnese to the Villa Farnesina. Nearby, the church of **Santa Maria dell'Orazione e delle Morte** (Holy Mary of Prayer and Death) has a facade of carved skeletal figures. The street is also home to many antique shops and furniture restorers.

Via Giulia • Bus: 23, 116, 280, 870

Piazza Navona

10 Piazza Navona is one of Italy's largest squares. Its oblong shape relates to the stadium built here by Emperor Domitian in the late first century A.D. The surrounding buildings, primarily from the 16th and 17th centuries, were sited on the footprint of the antique structure, whose ground floor now serves as their foundations. Pope Innocent X (1644–1655) is responsible for the square's current appearance, and the Palazzo Doria Pamphili, now the Brazilian Embassy, was his preferred residence. Next door, the church of **Sant'Agnese in Agone's** dome rises above the columns and towers of its white facade. Innocent X commissioned Francesco Borromini to design the church, but his rival, Gian Lorenzo Bernini, completed it. Bernini designed the central figure of "The Moor" for the square's **Fontana del Moro,** as well as the **Fontana dei Quattro Fiumi**. The latter is one of the city's most treasured fountains. Four marble sculptures of river gods—of the Nile, Danube, Tigris, and Plata—recline on a limestone grotto.

Piazza Navona • Bus: 70, 81, 116, 186, 492

Pantheon

*Rome's most intact ancient building remains one
of the world's most influential structures.*

The beam of light from the dome's oculus may have played a part in Roman ceremonies.

The Pantheon's name derives from the Greek *pan theios* (of all the gods), and
it may have served as a temple, though no one knows for sure. The current
Pantheon is the third such building to stand on the site—the previous two
were destroyed in fires. The structure, begun around A.D. 117 and completed
A.D. 126 to A.D. 128, was formed using a wooden frame to support poured
concrete. In 609, the Pantheon was consecrated as a church to the Virgin
Mary, which may explain why it is ancient Rome's best-preserved building.

■ THE DOME

Rising 142 feet (43.3m) above the floor (and spanning the same distance in diameter), the Pantheon's mighty dome is made from poured concrete mixed with stones. It is 20 feet (6 m) thick at the base and gradually gets thinner with height. Bronze once decorated the dome's recessed coffers, but this was stripped off in the early 7th century. Emperor Constans II removed the bronze on the dome's exterior in 663. At its center, a 30-foot-wide (9 m) hole, called the **oculus,** lets in light, air, and rain. When it's sunny, a breathtaking beam of light moves across the walls. When there's rain, a sheer sheet of droplets falls from the opening in what is one of Rome's most beautiful sights.

■ THE FLOOR

Very little of the building's original decoration survives; most of it was plundered in late antiquity and the Middle Ages. However, the floor's **geometric design,** made from colorful stones from Tunisia, Egypt, and Asia Minor, is original and was restored in the 19th century. Look for the **drainage holes** in the tiles beneath the oculus.

IN **THE KNOW**

The Pantheon's giant dome, which became a blueprint for so many buildings, remains the world's largest unreinforced concrete dome.

■ TOMBS

Like all Roman churches, the Pantheon has served as a cemetery. In a chapel to the left of the altar, Renaissance master **Raphael** is buried in a Roman sarcophagus. The 19th-century Queen Margherita—for whom the pizza is named—lies in the neighboring chapel with her spouse, King Umberto I. On the rotunda's opposite side is the **funeral monument of Vittorio Emanuele II,** first king of the unified Italy.

■ FACADE

The colonnade is made of 16 solid **granite columns,** 40 feet (12 m) tall. Above the colonnade, a Latin inscription states: "Marcus Agrippa the son of Lucius, three times consul, built this." Agrippa actually built the first Pantheon. The current building's patron—Emperor Hadrian—invoked Agrippa's name to link himself with an earlier period of imperial glory.

Piazza della Rotonda • 06 6830 0230 • Closed Jan. 1, May 1, and Dec. 25 • Bus: C3, 40, 46, 62, 63, 64, 70, 81, 87, 116, 119, 492, 628 • Tram: 8

The Piazza

Stop a moment in the Piazza Navona and what do you see? A school group scampers about with a soccer ball; a street performer tries to attract the attention of tourists; mothers push strollers, one hand on a cell phone; a priest hurries to a meeting; the clientele ebbs and flows beneath café umbrellas. All life is here, as it has been for centuries. A gathering place, an open theater of modern life—that is the nature of the Roman piazza, or square.

Piazza del Campidoglio, on the Capitolino, has distinctive geometric paving and building facades by Michelangelo (above). La Barcaccia in Piazza di Spagna marks a favorite meeting place (right).

Roman Origins

The Roman forum set the pattern for the piazza. Originally this was an outside meeting place, often for markets, which accrued a periphery of public buildings, such as temples, baths, or assembly halls. Italian architects in the Renaissance drew on Greek and Roman models when they contemplated how to design the "ideal city," and the public square was always a key, if not a central, ingredient.

The word "piazza" derives from the Latin *platea*, borrowed from the Greek *plateia* (broad). Thanks to the Romans, it's a word now seen in English, French, Spanish, and German as *plaza/place/platz*. The piazzas of Rome, however, are not sited on Roman forums or squares—they are largely Renaissance and baroque in origin. These parts of the city were main thoroughfares and so became prestige showpieces on which a great deal of artistic and architectural attention was lavished. As a result, many of Rome's piazzas and their attendant buildings were designed by the greatest architects and artists of the day—and remain some of the most impressive and most admired public spaces anywhere in the world.

Visual Splendors

Public sculpture is a feature of all Rome's piazzas, and the star is unquestionably Gian Lorenzo Bernini (1598–1680). He created, among others, the **Fontana dei Quattro Fiumi** in Piazza Navona (see p. 123) and Piazza Barberini's **Fontana delle Api** (Fountain of the Bees), utilizing the bee emblem of the Barberini family. His father, Pietro Bernini, designed **La Barcaccia** (the "Old Boat" fountain) in Piazza di Spagna (see p. 104). **Piazza del Campidoglio** (see p. 45), designed by Michelangelo, is an elegant space, with a copy of the second-century A.D. statue of Marcus Aurelius.

(see p. 123) ... (see p. 104) ... (see p. 45)

FIVE **TOP PIAZZAS**

Piazza delle Cinque Scole
Near a former Ghetto gate, and named for the five "schools" or synagogues in a house nearby.

Piazza Colonna Named for Marcus Aurelius's triumphal column *(colonna),* which has stood here since A.D. 193.

Piazza di Montecitorio
Bernini's design of 1650, now home to the Italian Parliament.

Piazza di Pietra An elegant square dominated by the ruins of the 2nd-century A.D. Temple of Hadrian.

Piazza di Sant'Ignazio
A masterpiece of rococo architecture, designed by Filippo Raguzzini in 1728.

Street Markets

Rome's 130 street markets come in two basic flavors: fresh produce and flea market. Each neighborhood has its own *mercato alimentare* (food market), which brings together the community every morning. Flea markets, usually held on Sundays, provide vintage fashion, funky home decor, and much more.

■ CAMPO DE' FIORI

This charming square (see p. 121) is best known for its effervescent nightlife, but it shows its most fragrant face in the morning with a fresh produce market. In the heart of Rome's historic center, this square became a hub of the city's commerce during the Renaissance, when it hosted horse traders. Today, the market is known for its stalls with jars, sacks, and containers full of herbs, spices, nuts, and dried fruits. Dazzling arrays of flowers and displays of fresh fruit and vegetables that change with the seasons offer a real feast for the palate and the eyes— and a good place to grab a picnic lunch.

Piazza Campo de' Fiori • Open 8 a.m.–2 p.m.; closed Sun.

■ BORGHETTO FLAMINIO

Located in a former bus garage, Borghetto Flaminio is one of Rome's chicest street markets, a short walk north of the Flaminio–Piazza del Popolo Metro station. The market aims to re-create the atmosphere of a Middle Eastern souk in the center of Rome. Borghetto has become the destination for sophisticated value shoppers looking for extravagant bijoux, vintage garments, second-hand bags of the finest brands, and much more. It's well known that Rome's ladies rent stalls here to get rid of their excess garments, bags, and accessories, and that newlyweds sell off their unwanted wedding gifts here.

Piazza della Marina 32 • 06 588 0517 • Entrance: € • Open Sun. 10 a.m.–7 p.m.

■ PORTA PORTESE

Every Sunday in Trastevere, Rome's largest flea market transforms the sleepy streets into an extravagant, loud, busy, and chaotic mosaic of stands. Stretching along Viale della Mura Portuensi to Porta Portese, this market

Campo de' Fiori translates as "field of flowers," referring to the square's origins as a meadow.

hosts more than a thousand stands that abound with everything imaginable: from Venetian carnival masks to vinyl records and Tiffany lamps. It takes some luck and talent to avoid buying a fake, or *la sòla* as they say in the Roman dialect. Presided over by the majestic Porta Portese gate, this popular market has become a Roman tradition and a brand, with countless cameos in Italian and foreign films alike.

Piazza Porta Portese • Open Sun. 8 a.m.–2 p.m.

■ ANTICAGLIE A PONTE MILVIO

The specialized antiques market at Ponte Milvio is sited 2 miles (3.2 km)

due north of Piazza del Popolo, on the north bank of the Tiber alongside one of its most majestic bridges. Ponte Milvio makes a romantic backdrop for browsing through furniture, statues, and paintings. More than 200 stalls offer valuable collectibles from porcelain dolls to art nouveau tea sets, and the market's excellent reputation for quality draws many antiques fans. It is particularly busy between March and November, when the warm sunshine entices both Romans and tourists outdoors for a Sunday stroll.

Piazzale Ponte Milvio • Open first and second Sun. of the month 9 a.m–8 p.m

Vaticano

The popes once ruled over the Papal States, a kingdom that stretched across the breadth of Italy. Today, the pope rules over the 110-acre (44.5 ha) Vatican City State—also known as the Holy See. His residence, audience halls, offices, and stupendous art collections (housed in the Musei Vaticani) are all contained within the Vatican City walls. The Musei Vaticani are open to the public, and millions of visitors pour in each year to enjoy such wonders as Michelangelo's frescoes on the Sistine Chapel ceiling. Piazza San Pietro, the only part of Vatican City not surrounded by a bastion wall, is the welcoming gateway into the Basilica di San Pietro (St. Peter's Basilica). Castel Sant'Angelo, formerly a papal fortress, lies just outside the Vatican walls to the east. The popes lost their political power and much of their property in 1870, when the Papal States fell to the Italian unification movement, and Vittorio Emanuele II became the king of a united Italy. For nearly six decades, papal authority was in limbo, until the Vatican City State was created with the Lateran Accord of 1929.

◗ **Night closes over the Tiber and the Ponte Sant'Angelo, with the dome of Basilica di San Pietro, designed by Michelangelo, rising in the background.**

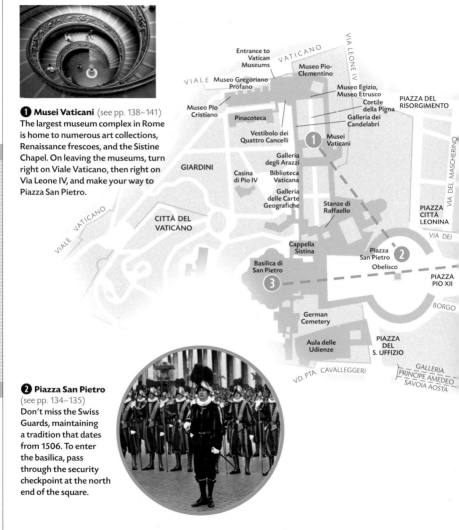

1 Musei Vaticani (see pp. 138–141)
The largest museum complex in Rome
is home to numerous art collections,
Renaissance frescoes, and the Sistine
Chapel. On leaving the museums, turn
right on Viale Vaticano, then right on
Via Leone IV, and make your way to
Piazza San Pietro.

VATICANO

Entrance to
Vatican
Museums

VATICANO

Museo Pio-
Clementino

VIA LEONE IV

VIALE   Museo Gregoriano
Profano

Museo Egizio,
Museo Etrusco

Cortile
della Pigna

PIAZZA DEL
RISORGIMENTO

Museo Pio
Cristiano

Pinacoteca

Galleria dei
Candelabri

VIA DEL MASCHERINO

Vestibolo dei
Quattro Cancelli

Musei
Vaticani

GIARDINI

Galleria
degli Arazzi

Casina
di Pio IV

Biblioteca
Vaticana

Galleria
delle Carte
Geografiche

Stanze di
Raffaello

PIAZZA
CITTÀ
LEONINA

VIALE   VATICANO

CITTÀ DEL
VATICANO

VIA DEI

Cappella
Sistina

Piazza
San Pietro

2

Obelisco

PIAZZA
PIO XII

Basilica di
San Pietro

3

BORGO

German
Cemetery

Aula delle
Udienze

PIAZZA
DEL
S. UFFIZIO

V.D. PTA. CAVALLEGGERI

GALLERIA
PRINCIPE AMEDEO
SAVOIA AOSTA

2 Piazza San Pietro
(see pp. 134–135)
Don't miss the Swiss
Guards, maintaining
a tradition that dates
from 1506. To enter
the basilica, pass
through the security
checkpoint at the north
end of the square.

VATICANO   **DISTANCE: 1 MILE (1.6 KM)   TIME: APPROX. 8 HOURS**
METRO START: OTTAVIANO, CIPRO, LINE A   BUS START: 23, 34, 40, 49, 62, 64, 280

Vaticano

The Musei Vaticani and Basilica di San Pietro brim with ancient, Renaissance, and baroque masterpieces.

```
0                     250 meters
0                     250 yards
```

VIA S PORCARI

VIA

PIAZZA A. CAPPONI

VIA G VITELLESCHI

CRESCENZIO

VIA DI PORTA CASTELLO

PIAZZA

ADRIANA

PIAZZA

VIA TRIBONIANO

ADRIANA

Castel Sant'Angelo

Leonine   Wall

CORRIDORI

BORGO SANT'ANGELO

VIA DI SANT'ANGELO

4

PIAZZA PIA

VIA DELLA CONCILIAZIONE

LUNGOTEVERE VATICANO

SANTANGELO

LUNGOTEVERE CASTELLO

PONTE

Pedestrian Zone

ANTO SPIRITO

PONTE VITTORIO EMANUELE II

Tevere

❹ **Castel Sant'Angelo**
(see pp. 136–137) Originally an emperor's mausoleum, the building was transformed into a fortress and, most recently, a museum.

❸ **Basilica di San Pietro**
(see pp. 135–136) The greatest church in Roman Catholic Christendom was designed by Bramante, Raphael, and Michelangelo and decorated by Bernini. From Piazza San Pietro, take Via della Concilazione to the end.

VATICANO

Musei Vaticani

See pp. 138–141.

Viale Vaticano 100 • http://mv.vatican.va • 06 6988 4947 • €€€€ • Closed Sun.,
Jan. 1, Jan. 6, Feb. 11, March 19, Easter Sun., Easter Mon., May 1, June 29, Aug. 14, Aug. 15,
Nov. 1, Dec. 8, Dec. 25, and Dec. 26 • Metro: Ottaviano, Cipro, Line A • Bus: 23, 34, 40, 64

Piazza San Pietro

The large, elliptical Piazza San Pietro (St. Peter's Square) in
front of the Basilica di San Pietro (St. Peter's Basilica) was laid
out by Neapolitan-born artist, sculptor, and architect Gian Lorenzo
Bernini for Pope Alexander VII from 1656 to 1667. Bernini's great
porticoes made from four rows of columns embrace the square like
welcoming arms, creating a space fit for tens of thousands of pilgrims.
Above the porticoes are 140 larger-than-life limestone saints, also
designed by Bernini. In 1586, before the square was built, Pope

Dominating Piazza San Pietro is Carlo Maderno's magnificent baroque facade for the basilica.

Sixtus V relocated an ancient Egyptian obelisk to its current site, centered in front of the basilica. The square is the usual setting for the pope's **general (public) audiences,** held every Wednesday, when he is in residence, usually at 10:30 a.m. He gives a short address to the crowd in at least six languages and delivers the Apostolic Blessing. On Sundays, when he is in residence, the pope appears at the window of his apartment at noon for the **Sunday Angelus,** giving a short blessing and addressing the crowd in the square.

W end of Via della Conciliazione • www.vatican.va • Metro: Ottaviano, Line A • Bus: 62

Basilica di San Pietro

3 Pope Julius II began the current basilica, the most important pilgrimage destination for the world's Roman Catholics, in 1506. It took more than a hundred years to complete—in 1612 under Pope Paul V. The new basilica stood on the site of a fourth-century predecessor, which was verging on collapse at the dawn of the Renaissance. According to tradition, the basilicas were built on the site where St. Peter was crucified and buried around A.D. 67.

"New" St. Peter's is massive, measuring 730 feet (222 m) in length, with a maximum height of 452 feet (138 m). The greatest architects of the Renaissance were employed in its design, including Donato Bramante, Raphael, and Michelangelo. For the **dome,** Michelangelo conceived a slightly pointed shape that exerted less thrust. This now-famous landmark was completed in 1590, 26 years after Michelangelo's death. Carlo Maderno finished the design of the basilica, extending the nave and adding the facade.

While Bernini decorated most of the interior in the baroque style (see pp. 82–83), several works of art were preserved from the old basilica, notably Michelangelo's **"Pietà,"** depicting the Virgin Mary mourning over the body of the crucified Christ. The statue,

SAVVY **TRAVELER**

Entry to papal general audiences is by ticket only. Tickets are free, available on-site from Swiss Guards one to three days in advance, or by reserving through the Prefecture of the Papal Household (*www.vatican .va/various/prefettura/ index_en.html*). Arrive early to get a seat—security checks begin around 8:30 a.m. No tickets are needed for the Sunday Angelus.

VATICANO

VATICANO

in the first chapel on the right, was made in 1498 by the 23-year-old Michelangelo, originally for a French cardinal. In the next chapel, the simple **tomb of Pope John Paul II** was consecrated on May 1, 2011. Beneath Michelangelo's mighty dome, Bernini's 95-foot-tall (29 m) canopy—the **baldacchino**—focuses attention on the **Papal Altar,** a white marble structure where the pope says Mass. Rising up into the massive vertical space of the dome, the baldacchino was Bernini's first work in the basilica, where he was engaged for six decades. Beyond the Papal Altar, the **Chapel of the Cathedra** is another glorious Bernini design in bronze and gilded stucco with an alabaster window. Its throne (*cathedra*) is a reliquary, believed to contain the remains of St. Peter's simple wooden throne. Bernini's last work inside the basilica was the **funeral monument of Pope Alexander VII** in the south transept. Alexander kneels in prayer, flanked by depictions of the virtues and accompanied by a bronze skeleton with wings, a symbol of mortality that implies Alexander's certainty of salvation.

Piazza San Pietro • www.vatican.va • 06 698 83731 • Metro: Ottaviano, Line A • Bus: 62

GOOD **EATS**

■ L'ARCANGELO
Chef Arcangelo Dandini prepares classic Roman dishes, including phenomenal gnocchi, in an elegant setting north of Castel Sant'Angelo. **Via Giuseppe Gioacchino Belli 59, 06 321 0992, €€€€**

■ LA PAIN À TABLE
Recharge with light meals, salads, and abundant vegetarian options between visits to the Musei Vaticani and the Basilica di San Pietro. **Via delle Milizie 13, 06 3750 0580, €€**

■ PIZZARIUM
Round the back of the Vatican, relish Rome's most famous pizza by the slice in an unassuming eatery. **Via della Meloria 43, 06 3974 5416, €**

Castel Sant'Angelo

4 This fortress on the banks of the Tiber— now home to the **Museo Nazionale di Castel Sant'Angelo**—has undergone several major transformations during its nearly 1,900-year life. It started as Emperor Hadrian's mausoleum, modeled on that of Augustus just across the river. In the Middle Ages, it was converted into a papal fortress named for St. Michael after a miraculous vision of the archangel was said to have ended an outbreak of the plague. In the 15th and 16th centuries, parts of the fortress were turned into residences for the pope and his court. It was also used as a prison, in

Statues of angels line the pedestrian-only Ponte Sant'Angelo, leading to the Castel Sant'Angelo.

which role it features in Puccini's opera *Tosca*—the heroine throws herself from the Castel Sant'Angelo's battlements in the last scene.

As you enter, take a look at the **Sala delle Urne** (Hall of Urns), on the second of the museum's seven levels. This housed the cremated remains (now lost), of Emperor Hadrian and his family. But the best part of the visit is in the upper levels. On the fourth, the **Sala Paolina** preserves sumptuous frescoes painted in the 1540s for Pope Paul III. On the upper level, the **Terrazzo dell'Angelo** offers panoramic vistas back toward the Basilica di San Pietro and across the Tiber, all under the presiding gaze of a huge bronze **statue of St. Michael.** Since the 1750s, this work by Flemish sculptor Pieter Anton Verschaffelt has topped the fortress as a reminder of the archangel's miraculous intervention.

Lungotevere Castello 50 • www.rome.info/vatican/castel-sant-angelo/ • 06 681 9111 • €€ • Closed Mon. and Jan. • Metro: Lepanto, Line A • Bus: 23, 34, 40, 49, 62, 280

Musei Vaticani

With 4.5 million visitors annually, the papal art collection is among the most popular tourist attractions in all of Europe.

Plato and Aristotle debate before an audience in Raphael's "School of Athens."

The Musei Vaticani (Vatican Museums) consist of different collections assembled over five centuries. Pope Julius II created the core by bringing together a group of ancient Roman statues, including the "Apollo Belvedere." The pieces were displayed for his visitors in his summer villa, the Belvedere Palace. Ideally, you would dedicate at least a day to the museums to begin to do them justice. A quicker visit, of around 2.5 hours, will include the Sistine Chapel, the Stanze di Raffaello (Raphael Rooms), and perhaps one other gallery.

PINACOTECA

The Pinacoteca (painting gallery) begins in the late Middle Ages and continues through the 18th century. Giotto's **"Stephaneschi Altarpiece"** (ca 1330) in Room II hints at the awakening of naturalism, which comes to fruition in Room IV with Melozzo da Forli's 15th-century fresco **"Sixtus IV Appoints Plotina Prefect of the Vatican Library."** In Room VIII, Raphael's **"Transfiguration"** (1516–1520) and his tapestries demonstrate the master's keen realism. Caravaggio's **"Deposition"** (ca 1600–1604) in Room XII employs a masterful use of light to great dramatic effect.

MUSEO PIO-CRISTIANO

The mosaics, reliefs, and sculptures in this collection of early Christian art show a distinct Roman pagan influence. Note how the **"Good Shepherd,"** a prototype for Christ, wears a tunic and resembles a beardless Greek god. Michelangelo emulated this in his Christ figure in the Sistine Chapel's "The Last Judgment."

MUSEO PIO-CLEMENTINO

This collection of ancient sculpture, one of several in the museums, contains major masterpieces, including works that influenced Michelangelo. The **"Apollo**

SAVVY **TRAVELER**

A one-way system operates within the museums, and there is a choice of four color-coded itineraries to follow, varying in length from 90 minutes to five hours. The Pinacoteca is located close to the entrance, and the Sistine Chapel and Raphael Rooms are about a half-hour walk from the entrance, not allowing for stops.

Belvedere" inspired the head of Christ in his "Last Judgment" in the Sistine Chapel, while **"Laocoön and His Sons"** provided the model for the Savior's legs.

MUSEO ETRUSCO

Founded in the 19th century by Pope Gregory XVI, the Etruscan collection owes its richness to the tradition of burying the dead with fine objects. Room II displays the findings from the **Regolini-Galassi Tomb,** discovered north of Rome in 1836. These include a gold fibula (brooch) from the seventh century B.C. In Rooms VII and VIII, luxurious gold jewelry attests to the wealth of the Etruscan civilization.

GALLERIA DEGLI ARAZZI

A long hall displays two cycles of tapestries (*arazzi*) on opposite walls. On the east side, the 16th-century **"New School Tapestries"**—so-called because they were made from designs

VATICANO

by Raphael's students—depict scenes from the life of Christ in intricate detail.

■ GALLERIA DELLE CARTE GEOGRAFICHE

On the west wall of the long Gallery of the Maps, Italy's west coast and parts of France are painted with brilliant accuracy. Facing them are the Adriatic coast and northern regions. The fresco to the right of the exit offers a charming view of Venice and its lagoon.

■ STANZE DI RAFFAELLO

The Raphael Rooms comprise four papal apartments redecorated by Raphael and his students for Popes Julius II, Leo X, and Clement VII. The **Stanza della Segnatura,** the third room, was Julius II's office. The walls embody his favorite subjects: jurisprudence, theology, poetry, and philosophy. On the eastern wall, the **"School of Athens"** depicts history's greatest thinkers debating and teaching in a fictional philosophy academy. Raphael painted himself into the image. He is on the far right wearing a red cloak and black beret.

■ COLLEZIONE ARTE RELIGIOSA MODERNA

The collection of modern religious art counts nearly a thousand works, which fill 55 rooms in the Borgia Apartments.

It includes Francis Bacon's **"Portrait of Pope Innocent X,"** a grotesque copy of Velázquez's painting, which hangs in the Palazzo Doria Pamphili (see p. 119).

■ CAPPELLA SISTINA

Rome's most significant artistic pilgrimage site, the Sistine Chapel, was built for Pope Sixtus IV from 1477 to 1481. Initially, the ceiling was painted blue with gold stars and the walls carried scenes from the lives of Moses and Christ. Sixtus IV called upon the greatest artists of his day, including Botticelli, to paint the chapel. And from 1508 to 1512, Sixtus's nephew, Pope Julius II, hired Michelangelo to replace the blue-and-gold ceiling.

For this colossal project Michelangelo designed and frescoed portraits of prophets , sibyls, Christ's ancestors, and scenes from Genesis. To view the images properly, stand near the western end of the chapel. They should be read from altar wall to entrance wall: "Separation of Light from Dark"; "Creation of the Sun, Moon, and Plants"; "Separation of Land from Sea"; "Creation of Adam"; "Creation of Eve"; "Original Sin and Expulsion from the Garden of Eden"; "Noah's Sacrifice"; "The Flood"; and "Noah's Drunkenness." For lay visitors these scenes visualized fundamental

Michelangelo's spectacular "The Last Judgment" fills the east wall of the Sistine Chapel.

principles about sin and divine primacy. The clergy, separated from the public by the rood screen, would have sat beneath images of the Creator, while the public, taught that they were wretched sinners, were associated with Noah, who survived the flood (an allegory for baptism) but later became drunk on wine, leading to humiliation.

On the ceiling above the altar, the prophet Jonah is a two-dimensional copy of the "Belvedere Torso" in the Museo Pio-Clementino. Below Jonah, the altar wall features **"The Last Judgment,"** which Michelangelo painted from 1537 to 1541. The saved surround Christ seated in judgment, while below him angels trumpet the arrival of the Apocalypse. The figures in the bottom left quadrant of the wall are also the saved; those on the lower left are the damned. Michelangelo's inspiration for the damned was not scripture, but rather Dante's *Inferno*.

Viale Vaticano 100 • http://mv.vatican.va • 06 6988 4947• €€€€ • Closed Sun., Jan. 1, Jan. 6, Feb. 11, March 19, Easter Sun., Easter Mon., May 1, June 29, Aug. 14, Aug. 15, Nov. 1, Dec. 8, Dec. 25, and Dec. 26 • Metro: Ottaviano, Cipro, Line A • Bus: 23, 34, 40, 49, 62, 64, 280

Legacy of the Popes

"On this rock I will build my church," Jesus says to St. Peter in the Bible, playing on the fact that the name Peter meant "rock." Around A.D. **67, St. Peter was martyred and buried on the Vatican Hill in Rome, in honor of which later Christian leaders decided to build the headquarters of the western Church there. St. Peter was declared the first pope (a word derived from the Latin** *papa*, or father), and there have been 264 popes since.

Raphael's portrait of Julius II scarcely reveals the fearsome temper of the *Papa Terribile* (above). Among many papal projects to beautify Rome was Innocent X's transformation of Piazza Navona (right).

Accumulating Power

It took nearly three centuries for Christianity to be officially recognized by the Romans, under Emperor Constantine, in A.D. 313. After the final collapse of the Western Roman Empire in 475 and of the Ostrogothic kingdom of Italy, which lasted until the mid-sixth century, the Roman Catholic Church provided continuity across Western Europe.

In 756, the popes became rulers of a swath of territory spanning central Italy—the Papal States. Here, they reigned like the kings and grand dukes of neighboring territories. The Vatican became their prime residence after the 14th century, but all Rome was their capital city.

Patrons of the Arts

The wealth and power of the papacy drew in the ruling families of Italy, such as the Della Rovere—glorious, capable, and often corrupt. During the high Renaissance, they made Rome the center point of art. Pope Julius II (1503–1513), a noted warrior, commissioned Michelangelo to paint the

Sistine Chapel ceiling and Raphael to adorn his apartments. He also founded the Musei Vaticani (see pp. 138–141), initially as a repository for the Roman antiquities rediscovered in the Renaissance. The popes' patronage spread to all the churches of Rome, as well as public buildings, monuments, and squares. Many popes—like Innocent X (1644–1655) when he transformed Piazza Navona into a baroque set piece—showed no shame in indulging in private projects.

The Protestant Reformation in the 16th century posed a direct threat to the papacy before the latter reasserted itself through the Counter-Reformation. This renewal was symbolized by the triumphant baroque style (see pp. 82–83) rolled out across Rome, remaining its hallmark into modern times.

MODERN **ART**

Unlike their predecessors, modern popes have not been in a position to be munificent patrons of the arts. But they have amassed an impressive **Collection of Modern Religious Art** (see p. 140), one of the best-kept secrets of the Musei Vaticani. Inaugurated in 1973 by Pope Paul VI, who hoped to encourage a renewed tradition of religious art, the collection consists of works donated by collectors or by the artists themselves. Highlights include **"Red Pietà"** by Marc Chagall, **"Christ and the Tempest"** by Giorgio de Chirico, and **"Ecce Homo"** by Georges Rouault.

Views of Rome

Extending over seven hills, Rome serves up lavish views of its terra-cotta roofs, bell towers, and cupolas from parks, church tops, and hilltop piazzas. Bridges over the Tiber also offer photogenic vistas, and many hotels have rooftop restaurants or bars where you can absorb the view accompanied by a flute of spumante.

VATICANO

■ CUPOLA DI SAN PIETRO

Having scaled the 320 stairs to the top of the great cupola of the Basilica di San Pietro (see pp. 135–136), you reap the reward of a breathtaking view. Below is **Piazza San Pietro.** Following the axis set by the red granite obelisk in the center of the square, your eye glides along the Via della Conciliazione, pausing at the **Castel Sant'Angelo** and the **Tiber.** The glory of Vatican architecture becomes self-evident.

Piazza San Pietro • http://saintpetersbasilica
.org/touristinfo.htm • 06 69 82 • €€

■ PIAZZA DEL CAMPIDOGLIO

The winning card of the Capitolino (Capitoline Hill), the lowest of Rome's seven hills, is neither Michelangelo's trapezoidal Piazza del Campidoglio (see p. 45) at its summit nor the equestrian statue of Marcus Aurelius. Instead, walk across to the square's eastern side, where a spectacular view awaits you: on the far left the **Fori Imperiali,** behind them the atmospheric Monti neighborhood, then the **Foro Romano** with the Temple of Saturn and the Arco di Settimio Severo, and finally the **Colosseo.** For further vistas, take a ride in a glass elevator to the top of the Vittoriano, next to the Campidoglio.

Piazza del Campidoglio

■ THE PINCIO

Although not among the seven hills, the Pincio (see p. 106), north of the Piazza di Spagna, offers superb views starting with **Piazza del Popolo** below. To the left lies the **historic center,** with the dome of Basilica di San Pietro beyond. In ancient times, noble families had gardens on the Pincio, hence its nickname, Collis Hortulorum (Hill of Little Gardens).

Access from Piazza del Popolo or Viale Trinità dei Monti

From St. Peter's cupola, looking over Piazza San Pietro, all roads seem to lead to the Vatican.

■ GIANICOLO

The vistas, peaceful atmosphere, and lush greenery of the Gianicolo (Janiculum Hill; see p. 153), on the west side of the Tiber, invite you to linger on this "balcony of Rome." Admire the **Basilica di San Pietro** to the left. Next comes the **Pantheon** and, to the right, the quaint **Trastevere** neighborhood. Numerous statues make this area an open-air museum, presided over by an equestrian bronze statue of Giuseppe Garibaldi, the hero of Italian unification.

Piazzale Giuseppe Garibaldi, NW of Trastevere

■ GIARDINO DEGLI ARANCI

On the top of the Aventino (Aventine Hill), south of the Ghetto, and facing the Tiber is one of the most beautiful gardens in Rome. The Giardino degli Aranci (see p. 168) was first laid out in the 14th century by the Savelli family. The Aventino, the most southerly of the seven hills, is off the tourist track, so you may have its views to yourself. Enjoying the shade of the orange trees, listening to cicadas, you'll understand why Rome is called the "eternal city."

Three entrances: Villa Balestra, Via di Santa Sabina, and Rocca Savella

Trastevere to Gianicolo

Trastevere lies across the Tiber River from Rome's historic center. In antiquity, the area was a blend of working-class housing and noble country villas. There were 13 synagogues, and early Christian communities were established here. Today, it is a compact residential district, with many of the medieval buildings resting on ancient foundations. The eastern part is quieter and artisans' shops fill the streets around Piazza di Santa Cecilia in Trastevere. The western side has wine bars, pubs, and restaurants, making it a major nightlife destination, the streets often packed into the wee hours. The Gianicolo (Janiculum Hill) rises above Trastevere, offering sweeping views over the city. Its leafy public gardens are peppered with monuments celebrating Italy's unification.

◐ **Trastevere's lively
squares and sleepy
lanes intertwine on
the slopes of the
Gianicolo, the city's
high spot.**

Trastevere to Gianicolo

Trastevere's meandering medieval streets give way to the verdant slopes and tranquil residential district of the Janiculum Hill.

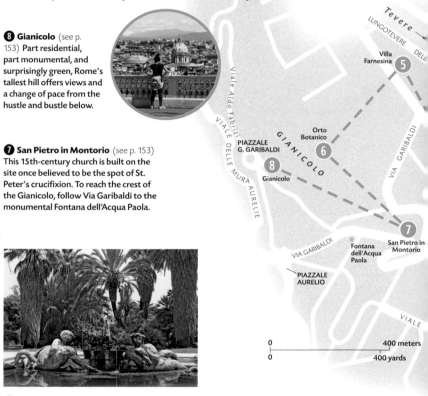

8 Gianicolo (see p. 153) Part residential, part monumental, and surprisingly green, Rome's tallest hill offers views and a change of pace from the hustle and bustle below.

7 San Pietro in Montorio (see p. 153) This 15th-century church is built on the site once believed to be the spot of St. Peter's crucifixion. To reach the crest of the Gianicolo, follow Via Garibaldi to the monumental Fontana dell'Acqua Paola.

6 Orto Botanico (see pp. 152–153) Rare plant specimens abound in Rome's botanical garden. Backtrack to Porta Settimiana, then pass beneath the arch, turn right, and ascend Via Garibaldi until you reach the church of San Pietro in Montorio.

5 Villa Farnesina (see pp. 154–155) A luxury villa built for a wealthy banker was decorated by Renaissance masters. Cross Via della Lungara, and take Via Corsini one block to the entrance of the Orto Botanico.

**TRASTEVERE TO GIANICOLO   DISTANCE: 2.5 MILES (4 KM)
TIME: 6 HOURS   BUS START: 23, 63, 280, 780**

1 Isola Tiberina (see p. 150)
This sandbar is the site of a famous hospital. Cross the Ponte Cestio into Trastevere, and at Piazza in Piscinula take the alley from the south of the square to Via del Salumi, turn left, then right on Via dei Vascellari. The church of Santa Cecilia is up on the right.

2 Santa Cecilia in Trastevere (see pp. 150–151) The medieval church celebrates a third-century virgin martyr. Exit the church complex and walk southwest on Via San Michele, turn right on Via Madonna dell'Orto, then left on Via Anicia.

3 San Francesco a Ripa (see p. 151–152) The complex was built around the convent where St. Francis of Assisi once stayed. Follow Via San Francesco a Ripa to the end, walk through Piazza San Callisto and into Piazza Santa Maria in Trastevere.

4 Santa Maria in Trastevere (see p. 152)
This mosaic-clad church dedicated to the Virgin Mary is one of the earliest Christian sites in the city. Exit the square from the west, and take Via della Paglia to Piazza Sant'Egidio. Walk north on Via della Scala, through the Porta Settimiana to Via della Lungara.

Isola Tiberina

1 Attached to the Ghetto and Trastevere by two ancient stone bridges, the Isola Tiberina is a natural sandbar that has gradually built up over the past 2,300 years. In 291 B.C., the Romans erected a temple to the healing god Aesculapius here and later outfitted its banks with limestone planks so it would resemble a ship, a playful allusion to the arrival of the Trojan hero Aeneas. In the Middle Ages, the church of San Bartolomeo was founded on the island. Its **12th-century bell tower,** a reminder of its origins, emerges from behind a restored 17th-century facade. Today, the adjacent monastery is home to a synagogue and a Jewish hospital, while the western side of the island is occupied by the Fatebenefratelli Hospital, famous for its obstetrics clinic. The lower banks, which have been extended and revetted in limestone, host summer events, including a film festival.

Between Ponte Garibaldi and Ponte Palatino • Bus: 23, 63, 280, 780

Santa Cecilia in Trastevere

2 A monumental gateway leads from Piazza Santa Cecilia in Trastevere into a medieval courtyard. The church of Santa Cecilia in Trastevere is dedicated to a virgin martyr who, according to tradition, was put to death on the site for her faith. The church itself is the product of three centuries of restoration from the 16th to the 19th centuries. The central vault and aisles are 18th-century restorations undertaken by Cardinal Acquaviva, but the magnificent **ninth-century apse mosaic** is original, showing a large-scale Christ flanked by saints. On the far left, St. Cecilia drapes her arm over the shoulder of Pope Paschal I, the ninth-century patron of the church. Unlike the other figures, he does not have a round halo, but rather a square nimbus, indicating he was still living at the time the mosaic was made. Beneath the main altar, Stefano Maderno's **sculpture of St. Cecilia** (1600) depicts her with her throat slit and a veil over her head. Her remains are in the crypt beneath the altar. Ring the

Stefano Maderno depicted St. Cecilia as she was said to have been found in her tomb.

bell at the convent beside the porch to visit Pietro Cavallini's **fresco of "The Last Judgment"** (1293).

Piazza di Santa Cecilia in Trastevere 22 • 06 589 9289 • Closed p.m. • Bus: 44, 23, 115, 125, 280, 780

San Francesco a Ripa

3 This Franciscan church was built in the 1230s on the site of the monastic complex where St. Francis of Assisi stayed during his visit to Rome in 1219. The church was given a baroque remodeling in the 17th century. In the left transept is Gian Lorenzo Bernini's masterful—and controversial—statue **"Beata Ludovica Albertoni"** (Beatified Ludovica Albertoni). She lies reclined on a bed with her eyes closed, clutching her body. The statue's erotic nature conflates the ideas of physical and spiritual pleasure in much the same manner

TRASTEVERE TO GIANICOLO

as the sculptor's "Ecstasy of St. Teresa" (see p. 76). The oratory houses the tomb of surrealist painter Giorgio de Chirico.

Piazza San Francesco d'Assisi 88 • 06 581 9020 • Bus: 23, 44, 115, 125, 280

Santa Maria in Trastevere

4 According to local lore, the church was built on the site of a miraculous eruption of oil in 38 B.C., where a Christian community was later founded. The current structure is a 12th-century rebuilding of the fourth-century original. The facade bears **mosaics of the Virgin Mary and the Infant Christ** flanked by virgins bearing gifts. The porch is an early 17th-century addition. Inside, the aisles are divided by granite monoliths that were taken from the Terme di Caracalla (see pp. 167–168). The church's masterpiece is its **apse,** a curving wall covered in gold and glass mosaics. Below, **Pietro Cavallini's mosaics** show scenes from the life of the Virgin (see p. 113).

Piazza Santa Maria in Trastevere • 06 581 9443 • Bus: 115, 125

SAVVY **TRAVELER**

Be sure to bring some coins to the church of Santa Maria in Trastevere. Feed the machine in the left aisle close to the main altar in order to illuminate the mosaics, which glimmer beneath the spotlights. Head to the left transept and central aisle for good views of the apse.

Villa Farnesina

5 See pp. 154–155.

Via della Lungara 230 • www.lincei.it • 06 6802 7397/7538 • Tours: e-mail lapenta@lincei.it • € • Closed p.m., Sun., and public holidays • Bus: 23, 125, 280

Orto Botanico

6 Rome's tranquil Orto Botanico (Botanical Gardens) climbs the slopes leading up to the Gianicolo from Trastevere. It occupies a 30-acre (12 ha) area that was once the garden of the neighboring Palazzo Corsini, a noble country villa. The gardens, which have been part of the University of Rome since 1983, are home to around 3,000 plant species, with specimens from around the world. The **bamboo grove, palm forest,** and **Japanese**

Garden showcase exotic species, while the **Bosco Mediterraneo** (Mediterranean Forest) is a collection of native varieties.

Largo Cristina di Svezia 24 • www.060608.it • 06 4991 2436 • € • Closed Sun., public holidays • Bus: 115, 125, 870

San Pietro in Montorio

7 This church was built in the late 15th century on the site erroneously believed to be where St. Peter was martyred. Inside, the first chapel on the right houses Sebastiano del Piombo's **"Flagellation of Christ with Sts. Francis and Peter."** In the cloister, Bramante created his masterpiece, the **Tempietto**, or little temple, in 1502. This circular, domed chapel surrounded by 16 Doric columns is of diminutive but harmonious proportions and is perhaps the most iconic building from Rome's Renaissance period.

Piazza San Pietro in Montorio 2 • www.060608.it • 06 581 3940 • Bus: 44, 75, 115, 125

Gianicolo

8 The tallest hill within the ancient city walls, the Gianicolo (Janiculum Hill) rises from the southern part of Trastevere. Climbing up Via Garibaldi, you find the **Fontana dell'Acqua Paola,** a fountain named for Pope Paul V and built to celebrate the reopening of an ancient aqueduct. Carlo Fontana added its huge basin in 1690. Continue along Via Garibaldi to the entrance to **Villa Pamphili,** Rome's largest public park. Northwest of the fountain, the Passeggiata del Gianicolo leads to an **equestrian statue of Giuseppe Garibaldi,** the general who brought about the unification of Italy between 1859 and 1870. There are panoramic views from the nearby belvedere.

Around Via Garibaldi • Bus: 115, 125, 870

GOOD **EATS**

■ **LA GENSOLA**
The specialty at this family-run restaurant near Isola Tiberina is fish done with a Sicilian flare, but the menu also features a selection of local Roman recipes.
Piazza della Gensola 15, 06 5833 2758, €€€€

■ **IVO A TRASTEVERE**
This busy pizzeria near Santa Maria in Trastevere serves thin and crispy Roman pies, as well as pasta and grilled meat dishes.
Via di San Francesco a Ripa 158, 06 581 7082, €

■ **LE MANI IN PASTA**
As the name suggests, pasta is the strong suit, but this popular restaurant near Santa Cecilia also serves excellent fish dishes.
Via dei Genovesi 37, 06 581 6017, €€€€

Villa Farnesina

Agostino Chigi's villa, outside the original city walls, features some of the Renaissance's liveliest and most amorous frescoes.

Raphael designed the ceiling frescoes of the villa's Loggia di Amore e Psiche.

A triumph of high Renaissance art and architecture, the Villa Farnesina was the country retreat of Sienese banker Agostino Chigi, one of the period's richest men. Completed in 1509, it was the crowning achievement of architect Baldassare Peruzzi. In the following years, the most innovative contemporary painters, including Peruzzi himself, decorated the interior, and elaborate gardens were laid out, dotted with pavilions and fountains. The property later passed to the noble Farnese family, for whom the villa is now named.

TRASTEVERE TO GIANICOLO

LOGGIA DI GALATEA

The Loggia di Galatea, "Hall of Galatea," the first room on the ground floor, owes its name to Raphael's fresco, **"The Triumph of Galatea."** This depicts Galatea, a beauteous sea nymph, waterskiing on a seashell pulled by dolphins. Tritons and other nymphs frolic around her, while above, cherubs with bows and arrows have her in their sights. The panel on the left shows her rejected—and dejected—suitor **Polyphemus** painted by another artist, Sebastiano del Piombo. Baldassare Peruzzi covered the vaulted ceiling with **constellation frescoes,** thought to represent Chigi's horoscope.

LOGGIA DI AMORE E PSICHE

Next door, frescoes inspired by the ancient myth of Amore (Cupid) and the mortal Psyche are the work of Raphael and his students around 1518. Scenes from their love affair are divided by garlands of fruit and vegetables, which include New World specimens depicted for the first time in Europe. The large ceiling panels show **"The Congress of the Gods"** and the climax of the love story, **"The Marriage of Cupid and Psyche."**

IN **THE KNOW**

During restoration of Peruzzi's trompe l'oeil columns in the Sala delle Prospettive, a piece of 16th-century graffiti in German was found. Left by a Lutheran invader at the time of Charles V's sack of Rome, it ridicules the pontiff: "1528—why shouldn't I laugh. The Landsknechts [mercenaries] have put the Pope to flight."

SALA DELLE PROSPETTIVE

Upstairs, in the great Room of Perspectives, Peruzzi painted an **illusionistic panorama of Rome** and the countryside beyond, seen through the trompe l'oeil columns of a loggia. This brilliant piece of visual deception shows his total grasp of perspective.

PRIVATE QUARTERS

Giovanni Antonio Bazzi (familiarly known as "Il Sodoma") decorated Chigi's private quarters with frescoes from the life of Alexander the Great. In **"Nuptials of the Conqueror and Roxane,"** cupids pull playfully at the clothes and sandals of the Persian princess Roxane as she awaits Alexander on their marriage bed.

TRASTEVERE TO GIANICOLO

Via della Lungara 230 • www.lincei.it • 06 6802 7397/7538 • Tours (reservation required): e-mail lapenta@lincei.it • € • Closed p.m., Sun., and public holidays • Bus: 23, 125, 280

Roman Food

Romans eat with gusto, dedicating quality time to the table. Indulging in the *cucina romana* (Roman cuisine) is as much a part of experiencing Rome as a stroll through the Foro Romano. Many of the city's restaurants stick close to tradition, serving classic dishes made with seasonal produce. Occasionally, visitors will encounter modern twists on Roman recipes, but even these stay true to the city's core gastronomic principles and ingredients.

The classic amatriciana sauce is served with long strands of bucatini or short tubes of rigatoni (above). Eating outdoors on a pretty side street adds to the gastronomic delights of lunch (right).

Four Courses

The Roman lunch and dinner may have as many as four courses: *antipasto* (starter), followed by *primo* (pasta), *secondo* (main dish, traditionally lamb or organ meats), and *dolce* (dessert).

Key Ingredients

Two ingredients make a regular appearance in Roman cuisine: *carciofo romanesco,* the local globe artichoke, and *pecorino romano.* Artichokes are prepared in two main styles: *alla giudia* (deep fried and seasoned with salt) or *alla romana* (braised with herbs and olive oil). *Pecorino romano,* also known as *cacio,* is a hard, salty cheese made with ewe's milk.

Quinto quarto, the so-called "fifth quarter," refers to Rome's organ meats tradition. In the 19th century, slaughterhouse-workers in the Testaccio district in the south of the city would receive part of their salary in poor cuts. Recipes for such foods developed in the local taverns. Look for stewed tripe, grilled sweetbreads, braised oxtail, and intestines cooked with pasta.

Pasta Medley

Favorite Roman pasta dishes include *cacio e pepe*—grated pecorino and black pepper, served with homemade *tonarelli* (fresh pasta strands). *Bucatini all'amatriciana* are thick, hollow spaghetti tossed in a tomato, *guanciale* (pork jowl), and pecorino sauce. *Carbonara*, served with a wider varity of pasta shapes, is a rich sauce of egg yolks, pecorino, and *guanciale*.

Perfect Pizza

The most popular pizza is undoubtedly *pizza bianca* (literally, white pizza), a flatbread brushed with extra virgin olive oil and seasoned with sea salt. It is enjoyed either as breakfast or as a snack, preferably from the authority, **Antico Forno Roscioli** (*Via de' Chiavari 34, 06 687 5287*).

DISH **OF THE DAY**

The "Roman culinary canon" calls for certain dishes to be prepared and eaten on designated days of the week. For example, the saying *"giovedì gnocchi"* (gnocchi on Thursdays) refers to the potato dumpling tradition. On Fridays, Romans eat fish, particularly *baccala* (salt cod), which falls in line with the Catholic calendar and Saturdays are for *trippa alla romana* (tripe stewed with mint and tomatoes and dusted with grated pecorino).

Rome by Night

Movida Romana—Roman nightlife—is legendary for its variety and high-octane beat. The most popular nightlife neighborhoods offer a wide choice for each phase of the evening: *aperitivo* (pre-dinner drinks), *cena* (dinner), *dopo-cena* (after-dinner drinks), and *divertimento* (entertainment or fun).

■ TRASTEVERE

This former neighborhood of artists and artisans has evolved into the beating heart of Roman nightlife. Affordable pizza places abound. A bar housed in a former garage, **Freni e Frizioni** (*Via del Politeama 4, 06 4549 7499, €€*) serves snacks and drinks from morning to late at night—don't miss its signature *aperitivo*. Finish off your evening at **Big Mama** (*Vicolo San Francesco a Ripa 18, 06 581 2551, €€*), the self-styled home of jazz and blues in Rome. A stalwart for decades, Big Mama still draws big, international acts and champions exciting young Italian talent. It's a very popular spot, so reservations are advised.

■ PIAZZA NAVONA
& CAMPO DE' FIORI

Near Piazza Navona and a few streets back from the Tiber, the traditional **Il Goccetto** (*Via dei Banchi Vecchi 14, 06 686 4268, €€*) takes up part of a medieval bishop's house. This wine bar still has the original painted ceilings and dark wood-paneled walls. The menu offers classic chiantis and proseccos as well as more unusual Italian wines from smaller vineyards, plus a wide selection of cheeses and cold meats.

When the sun sets, the fruit vendors and flower stalls of Campo de' Fiori (see p. 121) make way for fun-seeking multitudes. Two bars, **La Vineria Reggio** (*Campo de' Fiori 15, 06 6880 3268, €*) and **La Fiaschetta** (*Via dei Cappellari 64, €€*) offer a great wine selection and a lively atmosphere. Although Italian beer may not be as famous as German or Belgian brews, there is a flourishing community of artisan brewers. **Open Baladin** (*Via degli Specchi 6, 06 683 8989*), near the Campo de' Fiori, showcases the best of Italian beer with a selection of more than a hundred craft beers from across the country.

Renzo Piano's Auditorium Parco della Musica in the north of Rome was inaugurated in 2002.

■ TESTACCIO

The Testaccio area in southern Rome was once the home of railway depots, wholesale markets, and slaughterhouses. Many of these have been converted into dance clubs, galleries, and eateries. Before hitting the clubs, try **Perilli** (*Via Marmorata 39, 06 574 2415, €€€*) for true-to-the-bone Roman fare. At **Casa del Jazz** (*Viale Porte Ardeatina 55, 06 704 731, €€€*) big acts, such as Stewart Copeland, Eddie Palmieri, and Electric Hot Tuna, pull in big crowds to the indoor and outdoor concert spaces. The on-site restaurant offers some great licks, too.

■ MUSICAL NIGHTS

On stifling summer evenings, outdoor events become appealing. For classical music, the Terme di Caracalla make the most spectacular venue. Here, in the magical setting of the ancient Roman baths (see pp. 167–168), the **Teatro dell'Opera di Roma** stages performances from Verdi and Puccini to ballet, and innovative multimedia shows. At the futuristic **Auditorium Parco della Musica** (*Viale Pietro de Coubertin, www.auditorium.com*), the summer program includes a series of concerts ranging from pop and jazz to Latin and bluegrass.

The Ghetto to Testaccio

Several distinct neighborhoods hug a bend in the Tiber River just south of the city center. Opposite Trastevere, the Ghetto was a small, insalubrious neighborhood where popes once required Jews to live by law. The zone has been rejuvenated and a large synagogue celebrates the Ghetto's emancipation. Due south, the Teatro di Marcello entertained theater-goers in Roman times, and two temples from the Forum Boarium (Cattle Market) have survived relatively intact. Nearby, the large archaeological parks of Circo Massimo (Circus Maximus) and Terme di Caracalla (Baths of Caracalla) speak to the monumental nature of Roman architecture, while the adjacent Aventino (Aventine Hill) offers a quiet, shaded look at Roman life. Testaccio, at the bottom of the hill, is a modern residential district with a thriving commercial scene and nightlife.

◀ **The three pillars of the Tempio di Apollo rise up alongside Teatro di Marcello, with the synagogue in the background.**

The Ghetto to Testaccio

Follow the gamut of Roman history through archaeological sites to modern-day Testaccio.

❶ The Ghetto (see pp. 170–171) The Tempio Maggiore, a fine synagogue, presides over the thriving Jewish community. Descend into the ruins at Piazza 16 Ottobre 1943, and make for the curved facade of the Roman theater.

❷ Teatro di Marcello (see pp. 164–165) The facade of the ancient theater now supports residential housing. Ascend the ramp, and follow Via del Teatro di Marcello and Via L. Petroselli south to Piazza Bocca della Verità.

❸ Republican Temples (see p. 165) Two republican-era temples, among the oldest buildings in Rome, sit side by side amid the gravel and grass of a small park. Cross the street at the stoplight and enter the church porch.

❹ Santa Maria in Cosmedin & Bocca della Verità (see p. 166) Visit the medieval church and the Mouth of Truth, an ancient fountainhead and modern tourist attraction in the church porch. Then walk one block southeast.

❺ Circo Massimo (see pp. 166–167) A former chariot-racing stadium, the Circo Massimo has become a long, dusty field after centuries of floods and plundering. Exit at its southeastern end, and take the Via delle Terme di Caracalla 550 yards (500 m) to the entrance of the baths.

6 Terme di Caracalla (see pp. 167–168) Romans socialized for three centuries at the city's best preserved bathing complex. Backtrack to Circo Massimo, and ascend Via del Circo Massimo to Piazzale Ugo La Malfa. Take Via di Valle Murcia to Via di Santa Sabina.

7 The Aventino (see p. 168) A park filled with orange trees, the Santa Sabina church, and a keyhole with a view are all on Via di Santa Sabina. Take Via di Porta Lavernale downhill, and follow Via Marmorata southeast to Via Caio Cestio.

8 Protestant Cemetery (see pp. 168–169) The movers and shakers of Rome's non-Catholic community have been buried in this cemetery since the 18th century. Take Via Caio Cestio east, then make a right on Via Nicola Zabaglia and pass Monte Testaccio.

9 Testaccio (see p. 169) This 20th-century neighborhood known for its authentic cuisine and food market has been a hub of commerce since ancient times; see its commercial archaeology as well as the modern industrial ruins.

THE GHETTO TO TESTACCIO DISTANCE: 3.4 MILES (5.5 KM)
TIME: APPROX. 7 HOURS   BUS: 23, 40, 64, 87, 271, 571 • TRAM: 8

The Ghetto

1 See pp. 170–171.

Between Via del Portico d'Ottavia, Piazza delle Cinque Scole, and Lungotevere dei Cenci • Bus: 23, 40, 64, 87, 271, 571 • Tram: 8

Teatro di Marcello

2 Julius Caesar began ancient Rome's largest and most important theater around 50 B.C., and Emperor Augustus completed it after Caesar's assassination. Augustus named the theater, which he inaugurated around 13 B.C., for his deceased nephew Marcellus. The building's curving facade of stone arches, a third of which survives, became the model for the theaters and amphitheaters, including the Colosseo (see pp. 66–67), that spread throughout the Roman world. Up to 20,000 people filled the theater to watch dramas, comedies, and other performances until

In its heyday, the 108-feet-high (33 m) Teatro di Marcello had 41 arches over three stories.

the fifth century. In the 11th century, the building was transformed into a fortress, and in 1519 the architect Baldassare Peruzzi designed the Renaissance palace that can be seen superimposed on the structure. The upper levels, subdivided into apartments, are still inhabited. Walk past and gaze through the limestone arches leading to the passageways and staircases that the ancient Romans used to reach their seats for performances. Other nearby ruins include the **Portico d'Ottavia** (the entrance to a public complex), three marble columns from the **Tempio di Apollo,** the Greek god of healing, and the podium from the **Tempio di Bellona,** a warrior goddess. Summer concerts of classical music are held in the theater grounds.

Via del Teatro di Marcello • www.060608.it • Closed May 1 • Bus: 44, 81, 95, 271, 628

SAVVY **TRAVELER**

On Saturdays and Sundays, Via di San Teodoro 74, to the east of the Ghetto, hosts the **Mercato di Campagna Amica,** Rome's busiest farmer's market. Here you can browse the produce or purchase prepared foods to eat in the patio behind the market.

Republican Temples

3 The relatively well-preserved remains of two temples survive side by side in the shadow of Rome's ancient cattle market, the Forum Boarium. The rectangular **Tempio di Portunus,** dedicated to a harbor god and built in the fourth or third century B.C. from local tufa (volcanic stone), was covered by a layer of plaster to look like marble. Christians transformed the temple into a church in the ninth century, which guaranteed its maintenance. Likewise, the nearby **Tempio di Ercole,** dedicated to the hero and demi-god Hercules and made of Greek marble, survives because it became a church around the 12th century. The round structure, 49 feet (15 m) in diameter, is Rome's oldest marble temple, dating to the second or early first century B.C. Initially, it was erroneously identified as a temple to the goddess Vesta, but later found to be one of several sanctuaries in the area dedicated to Hercules, protector of the cattle market.

Piazza Bocca della Verità • Bus: 44, 81, 95, 271, 628

Santa Maria in Cosmedin & Bocca della Verità

4 The church of Santa Maria in Cosmedin was built by a Greek Byzantine community around the eighth century. Its porch is home to the **Bocca della Verità** (Mouth of Truth), an ancient Roman fountain with the head of a river god carved onto its surface in low relief. Legend holds that liars who put their hand inside the Bocca della Verità will be bitten by a serpent. Immortalized in such films as *Roman Holiday,* the Bocca della Verità draws thousands of visitors each day. The church itself is a magnificent work of medieval architecture, and its interior decor is an amalgam of repurposed Roman stone decorations, including a **12th-century mosaic floor** and the columns that divide the aisles.

Piazza Bocca della Verità 18 • www.060608.it • 06 678 7759 • Mouth of Truth: donation • Bus: 44, 81, 95, 271, 628

GOOD **EATS**

■ **AGUSTARELLO**
Popular with locals, this simple trattoria north of Testaccio serves typical Roman dishes, including hearty pastas, succulent grilled lamb, and offal. **Via Giovanni Branca 100, 06 574 6585, €€**

■ **CAFFÈ ST. TEODORO**
Pause in the shade and eat a sweet or savory snack, or even a light lunch, at this eatery near the Circo Massimo. **Via dei Fienili 51, 06 678 0933, €**

■ **FLAVIO AL VELAVEVODETTO**
Near Monte Testaccio, Roman dishes such as carbonara and oxtail are served in dining rooms adorned with fragments of ancient terra-cotta jugs. **Via di Monte Testaccio 97, 06 574 4194, €€**

Circo Massimo

5 According to legend, the kings of Rome inaugurated the Circo Massimo (Circus Maximus) in the sixth century B.C., but it's more likely the area didn't develop as a destination for public spectacle until the late republic. Chariot races, wild beast hunts, public executions, and gladiatorial combat entertained the crowds at the Circo Massimo, as politicians seeking to win the people's favor hosted games here. The seating consisted of three tiers, respectively of stone, concrete, and wood, and had a capacity of around 250,000 in the early second century A.D.—roughly five times that of the nearby Colosseo. Two ancient Egyptian obelisks, which now stand in Piazza del Popolo (see p. 105) and Piazza San Giovanni in Laterano (see p. 84), embellished a **long wall,** called the *spina,* dividing the track. After the circus fell out of use in the sixth century, flooding deposited silt, which covered the area. Most of the structure has been plundered, leaving a half-mile (1 km) circumference field in its wake. The circus is now a public park used for free concerts.

Via dei Cerchi and Via del Circo Massimo • www.060608.it • Metro: Circo Massimo, Line B • Bus: 81, 160, 175, 628 • Tram: 3

Terme di Caracalla

6 Ancient Rome's most opulent bathing complex, built between A.D. 211 and 216, is one of the city's best-preserved ruins. Bathers entered the Terme di Caracalla (Baths of Caracalla) from the northeast, left their belongings in the *apodyterium* (changing room), and began the bathing ritual in the circular *caldarium,* the very hot room. Next, visitors relaxed in the *tepidarium,* the lukewarm room, before cooling off in the *frigidarium,* where they would lounge by cold-water pools. This room is the only part of the bathing itinerary that is entirely accessible to visitors. Romans trained in

The lavish ancient leisure complex of the Terme di Caracalla now hosts a summer opera season.

the two symmetrical gymnasiums that flank the *frigidarium*. Finally, they would plunge into the *natatio,* an Olympic-size open-air pool, which is now a shallow indent in the ground. The other buildings around the bathing block may have been libraries and meeting rooms; all told, they could take 10,000 guests. Most of the marble and mosaic decorations have gone, yet the ruined walls give a sense of the baths' former grandeur. The **Teatro Dell'Opera di Roma** *(www.en.operaroma.it, 06 481 601)* holds an opera season here.

Via delle Terme di Caracalla 52 • www.archeoroma.beniculturali.it • 06 3996 7700
• €€ • Closed Jan. 1, Easter Mon., and Dec. 25 • Metro: Circo Massimo, Line B
• Bus: 118, 160, 175, 628 • Tram: 3

The Aventino

7 The Aventino (Aventine Hill), one of Rome's "seven hills," is a leafy residential district with wide-ranging views of the city. Head to the western outlook of the charming **Giardino degli Aranci** (Park of the Oranges) to sit among orange groves and look down on the Tiber River and Trastevere. Next to the park, the church of **Santa Sabina** dates from around A.D. 430 and represents one of the most pristine examples of the city's early Christian architecture. The church's wooden doors are original and include one of Rome's earliest depictions of Christ's crucifixion. In the next piazza, pause at the doorway of the Knights of Malta's palace and look through the **keyhole** to the palace gardens and the Basilica di San Pietro. Here you have the curious experience of being in Italy and looking through to two other countries: sovereign Maltese territory and Vatican City.

Between Lungotevere Aventino, Via del Circo Massimo, Via Marmorata, and Viale Aventino • Metro: Circo Massimo, Piramide, Line B • Bus: 60, 75, 81, 160, 175 • Tram: 3

Protestant Cemetery

8 Situated between the third-century Aurelian Walls, Piramide, and Monte Testaccio, the Protestant Cemetery was born of the need to provide burials for Rome's non-Catholic residents (despite its name, atheists, Jews, Muslims, and Orthodox Christians are also buried here). The cemetery, established in 1732 during the peak of the Grand Tour—an era in which many northern European and North American poets, artists, and scholars settled in Rome—has more than 4,000 graves. Noteworthy tombstones include those of English poet **John Keats** (1795–1821; see p. 105) and his friend and fellow poet **Percy Bysshe Shelley** (1792–1822).

Via Caio Cestio 6 •www.protestantcemetery.it • 06 574 1900
• Donation • Closed Sun. p.m. and public holidays • Metro: Piramide, Line B • Bus: 23, 30, 60, 75, 95, 175, 280 • Tram: 3

Graves of the literati in Rome's Protestant Cemetery include those of English poet Percy Bysshe Shelley (above) and American Beat poet Gregory Corso (1930–2001).

Testaccio

9 The 20th-century neighborhood of Testaccio lies between the Aventino and a curve in the Tiber River. Its buildings, mainly residential, are laid out in an organized grid system. Its main square, **Piazza di Testaccio,** is home to a covered food market that operates Monday through Saturday. In the southern part of Testaccio is an unconventional ruin—an ancient garbage dump that is now a 118-foot-tall (36 m) hill where trees and vines have taken root. Dubbed **"Monte Testaccio,"** the area is made from millions of discarded terra-cotta vessels once used to transport goods to ancient warehouses—the pieces were piled up from around 140 B.C. to A.D. 250. Today, restaurants, nightclubs, and even a mechanic shop have been built into the hill, whose significance was not realized until the 18th century. Next to Monte Testaccio, a slaughterhouse has been transformed into the **MACRO** (see p. 172), a venue for contemporary art exhibitions.

Between Via Marmorata, Lungotevere Testaccio, and Via Ostiense • Metro: Piramide, Line B • Bus: 23, 30, 60, 75, 95, 175, 280 • Tram: 3

The Ghetto

Though the Ghetto was abolished and the area rebuilt,
it remains the center of community life for Rome's 14,000 Jews.

Refined housing replaced the Ghetto's precarious dwellings in the 18th century.

During its 22 centuries in Rome, the Jewish community has been subjected to long periods of persecution. Pope Paul IV created the Ghetto in 1555, declaring it "absurd and improper" that Jews lived among Christians. He confined them to an area equivalent to four city blocks, stripped them of their rights, restricted their occupations, and severely limited their religious freedoms. Only when the papacy lost its political authority following Italian unification in 1870 did the Jewish community have its rights and citizenship restored.

■ IL FORNO DEL GHETTO BOCCIONI

The kosher bakery, Il Forno del Ghetto Boccioni *(Via del Portico d'Ottavia 1)*, is a Roman institution run by a slightly ill-tempered family known for lightly scorching their baked goods. In spite of it all, Il Forno's fragrant cinnamon biscotti, almond-paste cookies, ricotta cakes, and *pizza ebraica* (a dense candied fruit-and-nut loaf) enjoy cult status among Romans.

■ MUSEO EBRAICO

The Museo Ebraico (Jewish Museum) houses a collection of around 800 textiles from the Ghetto period in its first room. Renaissance velvets embellished with gold thread, baroque lace, and French 18th-century weavings are among the items on display. The rest of the museum documents the history of Roman Jewish life from antiquity to the present day, including the Libyan Jews who arrived in Rome in 1967 after fleeing pogroms in their home country.

■ TEMPIO MAGGIORE

A ticket to the Museo Ebraico includes a visit to the Tempio Maggiore (Great

IN **THE KNOW**

The Piazza 16 Ottobre 1943, a solemn square in front of the Portico d'Ottavia, pays tribute to Jews deported during the Nazi occupation. On the morning of October 16, 1943, Nazi forces entered the Ghetto and, going door to door, rounded up a thousand Jews, the majority of whom were women and children. More than 2,000 Roman Jews were sent to concentration camps across northern Europe.

Temple), the city's largest synagogue and the first building erected in the area after the end of the Ghetto period in 1870. The centrally planned temple, built by two Catholic architects in 1904 evokes church design. The ceilings are painted with symbols from the Old Testament: stars, cedars of Lebanon, and rainbows.

■ VIA DEL PORTICO D'OTTAVIA

Via del Portico d'Ottavia follows the Ghetto's former northern boundary. Today, its shops, kosher restaurants, and the Jewish day school all form the core of contemporary Roman Jewish community life.

Between Via del Portico d'Ottavia, Piazza delle Cinque Scole, and Lungotevere dei Cenci
• Museo Ebraico and Tempio Maggiore: Lungotevere dei Cenci 15 • www.museoebraico.roma.it
• 06 6840 0661 • €€ • Closed Fri. p.m., Sat., and Jewish holidays • Bus: 23, 40, 64, 87, 271, 571 • Tram: 8

Hipster Rome

Testaccio ranks high on the list of the city's ultra-cool neighborhoods. Elsewhere, too, winding streets are home to bars where art aficionados and movie buffs gravitate. There are galleries, themed clubs, and music-filled parks, and the latest highlight—MAXXI, the Museum of Art of the 21st Century.

■ MACRO

The Testaccio neighborhood's history parallels the evolution of New York's meatpacking district: slaughterhouse past, artists as a transforming force, and a lively present and future. With its youth-friendly opening hours (4 p.m. to midnight), MACRO Testaccio attracts university students and young professionals. The open spaces of the two key pavilions (beautifully refurbished ex-slaughterhouses) lend themselves perfectly to experimental art forms and create one of the most engaging architectural spaces in Rome.

Piazza Orazio Giustiniani 4 • www.macro.roma .museum • € varies per exhibition • Closed Mon., Jan. 1, May 1, Dec. 24–25, and Dec. 31

■ ROMA VINTAGE

During the summer days and nights, Parco di San Sebastiano, near the Terme di Caracalla (see pp. 167–168), entertains Rome's young and artistic crowd. Here visitors have free access to a variety of shows, from indie rock concerts to experimental theater, from revival dance nights to rockabilly parties and 1950s movies. Numerous food stands make this a full-day destination, especially on Sunday when the vintage flea market takes place.

Piazzale Numa Pompilio • www.romavintage.it • 06 574 3772 • Open mid-June–mid Aug.

■ MAXXI

In the Flaminio neighborhood, about a mile (1.6 km) north of Piazza del Popolo, you'll find architect Zaha Hadid's celebrated masterpiece, MAXXI (Museum of Art of the 21st Century). As you walk through the exhibition halls, drenched in natural light, the creative energy this space emanates becomes almost tangible. The busiest exhibitions are on architecture—no doubt because MAXXI is the first national museum

Art and architecture combine to make MAXXI top of Rome's hipster itinerary.

to focus on this specific domain. Don't miss the luminous cafeteria in the main hall, or the restaurant, **MAXXI21**(*06 320 7230, €€*), whose philosophy is *"kilometro zero"* and *"calorie zero,"* which means only locally grown ingredients are used and dishes come in at less than 250 calories each.

Via Guido Reni 4A • www.fondazionemaxxi.it • 06 3996 7350 • €€ • Closed Mon., May 1, and Dec. 25

■ Clubs & Watering Holes
Just a couple of blocks from Piazza Vittorio Emanuele II resides a bastion of the *"retrò"* scene, **The Micca Club** (*Via Pietro Micca 7a, 06 8744 0079*), inspired by the 1920s to 1960s in its programming and interior design. The club stages old-style variety, cabaret, and burlesque shows. East of the city center, Pigneto has emerged from a humble past to create a lively, varied dining and night scene. **Necci** (*Via Fanfulla da Lodi 68, 06 9760 1552*), a haunt of film director Pier Paolo Pasolini, is an endearing place to drop in for an aperitivo and homecooked fare. Nearby **Il Kino** (*Via Perugia 34, 06 9652 5810*) combines a bistro and biodynamic wine bar with a cinema showing independent movies, shorts, documentaries, and animation.

PART 3

Travel Essentials

PLANNING YOUR TRIP

When to Go

From May through summer, Rome's social life takes place outdoors. Restaurants and bars move their tables onto streets and piazzas, and there is a plethora of open-air cinemas and arts festivals. Many stores and restaurants shut in August, which, coupled with the intense summer heat, make this the least ideal month visit.

In recent years hotel prices have risen significantly, but discounts can sometimes be had in summer, as well as in January and February.

Climate

Rome has mild, damp winters; the temperature seldom drops below freezing and it rarely snows. Spring and fall tend to be rainy and warmish. Summer is dry and hot—often oppressively so in July and August.

Insurance

Take out enough travel insurance to cover emergency medical treatment, repatriation, and loss or theft.

HOW TO GET TO ROME

Passports

U.S. and Canadian citizens do not need a visa for stays in Italy of up to three months. By law, however, all visitors are supposed to announce their presence to the local police.

Hotels do this for you—leave your passport at reception when you check in and you'll get it back the following morning. You have to do this every time you check into a hotel, even if it's just for one night. Independent travelers and anybody staying for more than three months should contact La Questura, the central police station (*Via San Vitale 15, 06 46 861*), to find out what to do. In Italy you're meant to carry identification at all times—although you're unlikely to need to produce it.

Airports

Rome has two international airports: **Leonardo da Vinci—Fiumicino,** 18 miles (30 km) southwest of Rome; and the smaller **Ciampino,** southeast of the city. Both are run by Aeroporti di Roma (*www.adr.it, 06 65 951*). The website has transport information as well as real-time arrival and departure flight information, and other useful information. Ciampino currently services low-cost airlines, such as Ryanair and EasyJet, charters, and regional Italian airlines.

Getting to Rome center from Fiumicino airport

Two train services link the airport to central Rome. The **"Leonardo Express"** departs every 30 minutes from Termini station (5:52 a.m. to 10:52 p.m.) and from the airport (6:36 a.m. to 11:36 p.m.). The nonstop trip costs €14 and takes

about 30 minutes. The **FR1 train** to Trastevere, Ostiene, and Tiburtina costs €8 and departs every 15 minutes, from 5:58 a.m. to 11:28 p.m. For exact departure times, see *www.fsitaliane.it* (tip: To search, use "Roma" and "Fiumicino airport"). For transfers between 5:50 a.m. and 22:45 p.m., a bus runs between Fiumicino airport and Tiburtina station (*www.cotralspa.it, 06 7205 7205*).

Getting to Rome center from Ciampino airport

Several companies link the airport to Rome's Termini station. Allow at least three hours before flight departures; the bus journey to the airport takes around 45 minutes. **Sitbus shuttle** (*www.sitbusshuttle.it, 06 591 6826*) leaves Termini from 6:30 a.m. to 11:30 p.m., and from Ciampino, 7:45 a.m. to 11:15 p.m. It costs €6. **Terravision** (*www.terravision.eu, 06 9761 0632*) times its departures to coincide with flights and is restricted to passengers flying on certain airlines. It costs €4. The **Cotral** bus company (*www.cotralspa.it, 06 7205 7205*) runs a service until 11:45 p.m. to Termini station. It costs €6. The company also runs a shuttle service to Anagnina Metro station, Line A.

By Taxi

The city has set standard fares to and from the

airports. A taxi from Fiumicino airport to central Rome costs €40, and from Ciampino airport €30.

By Limousine & Shuttle

A limousine service to Rome's airports and other cities in Italy is offered by **Airport Connection Service** (*www.air portconnection.it, 06 338 3221*). They pick up and drop off at any address. If you are alone with luggage, **Airport Shuttle** (*www.airportshuttle.it, 06 4201 3469*) is a useful service, picking up and dropping off at specific addresses. **Rome Airport Shuttle** (*www.rexervation.com/ shuttleservice.asp, 06 9774 5497*) runs between Fiumicino airport only and most hotels, leaving every 30–40 minutes from 7:45 a.m. to 10:15 p.m.

GETTING AROUND ROME

Public Transportation

Buses, trams, the Metro, and local rail services in Rome are all integrated into one transport system. Tickets can be bought at most tobacconists, some newsstands, train stations, and at machines placed at key locations (go to "tickets and passes" on the English-language version of *www.atac.roma.it* for a list). Some new buses have ticket-dispensing machines but as these are unreliable, it's best to buy tickets before boarding. An ordinary ticket (BIT—*biglietto integrato a tempo,* €1) entitles you to 75 minutes of unlimited bus and/or tram travel plus one journey by train or metro. A day pass (BIG—*biglietto integrato giornaliero,* €4) is valid until midnight. A three-day tourist pass (BTI—*biglietto turistico integrato,* €11) is good until midnight of the third day after purchase. Also available is a weekly pass (CIS—*carta integrata settimanale,* €16).

All tickets must be validated at the beginning of your first ride and again if you switch to the Metro or vice versa. Machines for doing this are on buses or at the entrance to Metro and train stations. Keep the validated ticket until the end of your journey in case you are queried by an inspector. Traveling without a valid or a validated ticket makes you liable to pay a fine of at least €50.

Metro

The Rome subway, where many stations have been spruced up with original mosaics by top contemporary artists, operates from 5:30 a.m. to 11:30 p.m. (until 12:30 a.m. on Saturday). Rome has only two subway lines (A and B), which cross at Termini and only go to limited areas of the city.

Buses & Trams

The transport network, ATAC, has a vast bus and tram system, which can take you almost anywhere in the city (at peak hours travel times can be lengthy). On weekdays lines run until midnight or 12:30 a.m.; there are several nighttime, or *notturni,* lines as well.

Taxis

Taxis are available at taxi stands, and are generally painted white or yellow, with signs saying "Taxi." It can be difficult to hail a taxi in the the street, and by law they are not allowed to pick you up within 328 feet (100 m) of a stand. When a cab is free the "taxi" sign on the roof is lit up. Taxis run on meters, which start at €2.80 and increase every 0.6 mile (1 km) or 20 seconds. On Sundays/holidays, the beginning fare is €4, and at night (10 p.m. to 7 a.m.) €5.80. The first piece of baggage is free; each additional bag costs €1. Travelers who start their journey at Termini station must pay an additional €2. By law, fares must be clearly displayed. Tipping is optional but a good idea if you ask for added help with your baggage.

Trains

Trains to other cities in Lazio or the rest of Italy leave from either Termini or Tiburtina stations. Tickets can also be bought from selected travel agencies or direct from Trenitalia (*www.trenitalia.it, 89 20 21 or 06 6847 5475*), who also have information on Eurostar or Intercity reservations and purchases. Eurostar and Intercity train tickets can now be bought up to 10 minutes before departure if seats are available. Unless you're traveling by Eurostar, remember that before boarding you must punch your ticket in one of the yellow punch boxes scattered throughout the station.

Tours & Sightseeing

Independent sightseeing

Unless you're short on time, Rome is easy to visit on your own. The key is flexibility. In general, archaeological sites are open the whole day, closing an hour before sunset. Museums sell their last tickets an hour before closing. Churches usually close from noon to 3 p.m. and then for the night at around 7 p.m. The Rome Tourist Office (*www.060608.it, 06 0608*) can provide information, in English, about events, hours, and transport (press "2" for an English-speaking operator). There are also a dozen information centers in green kiosks around the city.

Reservations for most museums and archaeological sites can be made through Pierreci (*www.pierreci.it, 06 3996 7700*).

Bus tours

Trambus Open (*www.tram busopen.com, 800 281281*), run by the city of Rome, offers moderately priced bus tours that allow you to hop on and off at any of the stops all day. The buses, equipped with audio guides, start from Piazza dei Cinquecento (Termini station), and tickets can be bought at the Trambus Open info box in Piazza dei Cinquecento, at Trambus Open authorized dealers, and online.

Walking tours in English

Private walking tours are conducted by **In Italy's Companions** (*www.initaly .com, tel in U.S. 877 655 9221*).

Context Travel (*www.context travel.com, tel in U.S. 215 240 4347*) offers tours of the historic center.

Bicycle & Scooter Rental

Rome has about 100 miles (160 km) of bike paths, and many companies rent bikes and scooters. The most convenient are **Scooter Rent** at Termini Station (*to the right of Piazza dei Cinquecento, www.trenoescooter .com, 06 4890 5823*) and **Bici & Baci** (*Via del Viminale 5, www .bicibaci.com, 06 482 8443*).

PRACTICAL ADVICE

Electricity

Nearly all Italian circuits use 220 volts; American appliances need adapter plugs, and those that operate on 110 volts will also need a transformer.

Internet Cafés

These can be hard to find, but **Il Mastello** (*Via San Francesco a Ripa 62, 7 a.m. to 10:30 p.m.*), **La Casa del Caffè Tazza D'Oro** (*Via dei Pastini 2*), and **Internet Café** (*Via dei Marrucini 12*) are all good choices. If you have your own laptop with a wireless card, you will be able to access the Internet from the many cafés and public places that now offer free WiFi connections. To find public places where you can access the Internet, see *www.romawireless.com*.

Money Matters

Banca Intesa, *Via del Corso 226, 06 67121*.
American Express, *Largo Caduti di El Alamein 9, 06 722 801*.
Banca Nazionale del Lavoro (BNL), *Via Bissolati 2 (Piazza Barberini), 06 47031*.

To change money, go to a major bank or a store-front exchange office (look for the *"cambio"* sign). For the best exchange rate, however, use your debit or credit card at one of the many ATMs in the city.

National Holidays

Jan. 1, Jan. 6, Easter Sun., Easter Mon., April 25, May 1, June 2, June 29 (Rome only), Aug. 15, Nov. 1, Dec. 8, Dec. 25, Dec. 26.

Opening Times

Hours in Rome can be erratic, making sightseeing and shopping difficult. Shops in areas like Trastevere or Testaccio tend to close at lunchtime (generally 1 or 1:30 p.m.–3:30 or 4 p.m.) so be sure to phone first to check. Most Italian banks are open 8:30 or 8:45 a.m.–1:30 p.m. and 2:45–4:15 p.m. Mon.–Fri.; a very few are also open Saturday mornings. Many clothing stores are closed on Monday mornings. Supermarkets often open on Sundays although most independent shopkeepers prefer to take the day off.

Bars open in the early morning; some close at 8 p.m. but many in the center stay open until midnight or 2 a.m. Traditional restaurants generally serve between 12:30 and 3 p.m. and from 8 to 11 p.m., but some areas, such as Trastevere, have many restaurants that open at noon and stay open all day. Many businesses close for the August holiday, some for half, some for the whole month.

Restrooms

Rome has few public restrooms, but bars and cafés must let you use theirs. One toilet often serves both men and women. Standards of hygiene vary and it's a good idea to carry tissues, as toilet paper isn't guaranteed.

Telephones

To call Italy from the United States, dial 011 39 (international and Italian country code) then the local number, which always includes the city area code: 06 for Rome. This goes for in-city calls as well. Be aware that, not counting the area codes, Italian phone numbers can have from four digits (government offices, some embassies) to eight digits. 800 and 848 numbers are toll free. 199 numbers have a higher rate. For directory assistance, call 1254. To make a collect call, dial 170. Public phones are operated by phone cards, which can be bought from tobacconists, bars, and post offices.

Time Differences

Italy is six hours ahead of New York, nine hours ahead of Los Angeles, and one hour ahead of London. In Europe, clocks move forward one hour on the last Sunday of March and return to standard time on the last Sunday in October.

Travelers with Disabilities

Rome is not an easy city for people with disabilities. Most museums now have wheelchair-accessible bathrooms and stair lifts, but the entrances and exits of many museums, shops, restaurants, and hotels have not yet been made accessible. The Musei Vaticani, which have ten wheelchairs available at its Guardaroba (cloakroom), is a notable exception. Many sidewalks in Rome lack curb cuts or ramps, and those that exist are often steep. Stair lifts in museums and churches tend to be smaller and have a lower weight capacity than those in the U.S. There are elevators at all the Metro stations on line B except for Circo Massimo, Colosseo, and Cavour. Only Cipro (Vatican) and Valle Aurelia have elevators on line A. A reliable but expensive private van service is **Fausta Trasporti** (www.faustatrasporti .it, 06 503 6040). Free guided tours, in English, for disabled persons are available through **CO.IN**, but book early (800 271027). **Context Travel** (see p. 178) offers a specially designed program for travelers with mobility issues.

EMERGENCIES

Embassies & Consulates

British embassy Via XX Settembre 80/A (Porta Pia), 06 4220 0001, Bus: 16, 36, 60, 61, 62, 84, 90, 492.
Canadian embassy and consulate, Via Zara 30,

06 85444 2911 or 06 854 441 (24-hour emergency service), Metro: Bologna, Policlinico, Line B, Bus: 36, 60, 62, 84
United States embassy, Palazzo Margherita, Via Vittorio Veneto 119/A, 06 46 741, Metro: Barberini, Line A, Bus: 53, 63, 80, 95.
United States consulate, Via Vittorio Veneto 121, 06 46 741.

Emergency Phone Numbers

Police, tel 112
Fire, tel 115
Ambulance/emergency medical assistance, tel 118

Nighttime Pharmacies

Farmacia della Stazione, Piazza dei Cinquecento 49, 06 488 0019, Open 24/7
Farmacia Internazionale, Piazza Barberini 49, 06 487 1195
Farmacia Piazza Bologna, Piazza Bologna 20, 06 488 0754, Open 24/7
Farmacia Piram, Via Nazionale 228, 06 488 0754
Vatican Pharmacy, Via di Porta Angelica (enter Vatican at the Porta Sant'Anna entrance, 06 686 4146, nighttime opening Sat. only, 7:30 a.m.–1 p.m. Bus: 23, 49, 51) has an English-speaking staff.

Lost Property

For items lost on public transportation or anywhere else in the city, call this office before visiting:
Oggetti Smarriti, Via Prospero Alpino 63A, 06 6769 3214, Open 8:30 a.m.–1 p.m. Mon. to Fri., 8:30 a.m.–5 p.m. Thurs., Metro: Garbatella, Line B, Bus: 716

HOTELS

Rome is not particularly known for its excellent accommodations, yet both luxurious and charming places do exist, from antique-filled palaces old and new, to more intimate family-run establishments. Take your time to do a little research, using this list as a starting point. Rome is quite a small city, so you're unlikely to be too far from the main tourist sites, but if you're short on time, try to stay as close as possible to where you want to visit. Hotels can be very expensive, but it is worth looking out for deals, even in season—to benefit from these, you will usually need to reserve in advance via their websites.

TRAVEL ESSENTIALS

Given the relative scarcity of good, reasonably priced accommodation in Rome, it is best to reserve as much in advance as possible to secure your preference. You'll probably be asked for a deposit or credit card number. Many hotels do not take American Express or Diners Club, so check if you are planning to pay your final bill with either of those cards.

Central Rome (especially Trastevere and the areas around Piazza Navona and Campo de' Fiori) is noisy until 2 or 3 a.m. every night. If you're booking in these areas ask for a quiet room—and consider earplugs. Remember, too, that many of the older hotels in the city have fairly small rooms, so ask to look first.

Few hotels have rooms that are specially adapted for disabled travelers, but many will do all they can to accommodate special needs, especially if you let them know in advance.

Street parking is extremely difficult to find in the historic center, but most hotels will help you and arrange for you to use a garage—for which you will usually have to pay an additional daily charge. It's a good idea to inquire in advance about parking if you know you're going to need it, although driving in Rome is not particularly recommended.

Grading System

Italian hotels are rated from one to five stars by the Government's Tourist Office according to such facilities as the number of rooms with private bathrooms, and rooms with TV and other amenities, rather than style or comfort. However, this is not always a reliable measure as, for tax reasons, many hotels opt to stay in a lower category. Unless otherwise noted, all the hotels listed here have private bathrooms in all rooms (upper categories have bathtub and shower; lower, only shower). English is spoken at all the hotels listed, but the amount spoken varies and may only be sufficient to take a booking and deal with the most basic visitor requests. Value-added tax and service are included in the prices, and so is breakfast, unless otherwise noted. Room price categories are given only for guidance and do not take account of seasonal variations.

Alternative Accommodations

Many Roman monasteries and convents have comfortable rooms to rent at reasonable prices. See www.santasusanna .org, www.monasterystays.com, and www.hospites.it, for more information.

For short-term apartment rentals, check out www.vrbo.com, www.vacationrentals.com, and www .romaclick.com.

Organization

Hotels listed here have been grouped first according to neighborhood, then listed alphabetically by price range.

Price Range

An indication of the cost of a double room in the high season is given by € signs.

€€€€€	Over €320
€€€€	€250–€320
€€€	€175–€250
€€	€85–€175
€	Under €85

Text Symbols

ⓘ No. of Guest Rooms
🚇 Public transportation Ⓟ Parking
🛗 Elevator ❄ Air Conditioning
🏋 Health Club 🏊 Outdoor
Pool ⊕ Closed 💳 Credit Cards

ANCIENT ROME

Until a few years ago, the Monti area (which straddles the lower end of Via Cavour) was busy during the day but quiet in the evening. Yet Monti, now full of bars, pubs, and restaurants, has become a nighttime destination.

🚇 Metro: Barberini, Line A
• Bus: 60, 75, 84, 85, 87

■ Inn at the Forum
€€€€€
VIA DEGLI IBERNESI 30
TEL 06 6919 0970
www.theinnattheroman
forum.com

Just a few steps from the Foro Romano, this luxury hotel actually houses Roman ruins. Three of the rooms have terraces overlooking a little, tree-shaded garden—a lovely spot for an evening drink.

🛈 12 ⬆ 🅢 🕸 All major cards

■ Forum
€€€
VIA TOR DE' CONTI 25
TEL 06 679 2446
www.hotelforumrome.com

Tucked in a quiet corner behind the Fori Imperiali, the decor and atmosphere of this grand hotel are reminiscent of an English gentlemen's club. Rooms vary in size, but all are well furnished.

🛈 80 🅿 ⬆ 🅢 🕸 All major cards

■ Richmond
€€€
LARGO C. RICCI 36
TEL 06 6994 1256
www.hotelrichmond
roma.com

This small, family-run hotel is well placed for sight-seeing. The rooms are simple and well equipped. In summer breakfast is served on a terrace with great views over the Fori Imperiali.

🛈 13 🅿 ⬆ 🅢
🕸 All major cards

■ Nerva
€€
VIA TOR DE' CONTI 3
TEL 06 679 3764
www.hotelnerva.com

This friendly hotel, situated just steps from the Roman Forum, underwent a recent renovation. The public areas are pleasingly decorated and the rooms comfortable and sound-proofed.

🛈 18 🅿 ⬆ 🅢 🕸 V, DC

COLOSSEO TO SAN PIETRO IN VINCOLI

The streets around the Colosseum, particularly Via Capo d'Africa, have undergone a renaissance. New hotels have opened, innovative restaurants thrive, and bars stay open until the early hours of the morning.

🚇 Metro: Colosseo, Line B • Bus: C3, 60, 75, 81, 85, 87, 175, 673

■ Palazzo Manfredi
€€€€€
VIA LABICANA 125
TEL 06 7759 1380
FAX 06 700 5638
www.hotelgladiatori.it

An elegant hotel facing the Colosseo and next door to the ancient gladiators' training ground. The rooms are tastefully decorated. The roof terrace offers spectacular views, especially at sunset, and at night.

🛈 17 🅿 (extra) ⬆ 🅢
🕸 All major cards

■ Celio
€€€
VIA DEI SANTI QUATTRO CORONATI 35/C
TEL 06 7049 5333
FAX 06 709 6377
www.hotelcelio.com

Located in an 1870 mansion on a quiet street near the Colosseo, this family-run hotel has been recently refurbished and is one of Rome's most pleasant. The spacious rooms are frescoed with reproductions of Renaissance and baroque works, and the upper floors have jacuzzis. Breakfast is served in the rooms and on the terrace.

🛈 20 🅿 (extra) ⬆ 🅢 🔟
🕸 All major cards

■ Capo d'Africa
€€
VIA CAPO D'AFRICA 54
TEL 06 772801
FAX 06 7728 0801
www.hotelcapodafrica.com

Located in the shadow of the Colosseo, this four-star hotel is a fusion of contemporary and classic styles. The rooms have been furnished with great attention to detail. There is a wonderful view of the Colosseo from the terrace. Breakfast is extra.

🛈 64 🅿 (extra) ⬆ 🅢 🔟
🕸 All major cards

LATERANO TO TERME DI DIOCLEZIANO

Although the area immediately around Termini, the central train station, is probably best avoided at night, the atmosphere changes quickly as you venture slightly farther out. Here you will find hotels and restaurants ranging from the simple to the most luxurious. For public transport, see individual listings.

■ Grand St. Regis
€€€€€
VIA V. E. ORLANDO 3
TEL 06 47 091
FAX 06 474 7307
www.stregis.com
A traditional luxury hotel with public rooms that are decorated with marble columns and richly patterned Oriental carpets. The spacious and comfortable guest rooms are furnished with valuable antiques, and the bathrooms are well-equipped. Its highly recommended restaurant, Vivendo, serves traditionally innovative dishes in an exclusive ambience.

ⓘ *138 plus 23 suites* 🚇 *Metro: Repubblica, Line A* • *Bus: 60, 61, 62, 84, 175, 492, 590, 910* 🅿 *Garage* 🔄 🔟 🕐 *Closed Sat. L & Sun.* 🔷 *All major cards*

■ Radisson Blu
€€€€
VIA FILIPPO TURATI 171
TEL 06 444841
FAX 06 4434 1396
www.radissonblu.com
Though not in the nicest part of town, this minimalist-style hotel is conveniently located close to the central train station. It has individually designed guest rooms on seven floors, two restaurants, and a roof terrace with swimming pool. Breakfast is extra.

ⓘ *232 plus 26 suites* 🚇 *Metro: Vittorio Emanuele, Line A* • *Bus: 70, 71* 🅿 *(extra)* 🔄 🔟 📺 🏊 🔷 *All major cards*

THE QUIRINALE TO VIA VENETO

Many of Rome's luxury hotels can be found on the Via Vittorio Veneto, made famous by Fellini's film *La Dolce Vita*. Although the glamour of the 1950s is gone, there are plans to revitalize the area.

🚇 *Metro: Barberini, Line A* • *Bus: 52, 60, 61, 62, 63, 80, 95, 116, 175, 492, 590*

■ Eden
€€€€€
VIA LUDOVISI 49
TEL 06 478121
FAX 06 482 1584
www.edenroma.com
This luxury hotel is a favorite among international celebrities. Every detail is captivating, from the antique furnishings to the imaginative welcome baskets. The famous roof terrace offers stunning views. Breakfast is extra.

ⓘ *121, including some suites* 🅿 *Garage* 🔄 🔟 🔷 *All major cards*

■ Aleph
€€€€
VIA SAN BASILIO 15
TEL 06 422901
FAX 06 4229 0000
www.aleph.boscolo
hotels.com
This luxury hotel, of the Boscolo chain, was created by the Israeli architect Adam Tihany. In public spaces the theme is paradise to purgatory, while the guest rooms are decorated in contemporary style. The Seventh Heaven roof terrace is ideal for relaxing after shopping or sightseeing, and there is a spa. Breakfast is extra.

ⓘ *96* 🅿 *(extra)* 🔄 🔟 🔷 *All major cards*

■ Westin Excelsior
€€€€
VIA VITTORIO VENETO 125
TEL 06 47081
FAX 06 482 6205
www.starwoodhotels.com/westin
This dramatically grand hotel is opulently decorated with swaths of rich fabric and antique and reproduction furniture. All the more-or-less uniformly decorated rooms are luxurious, while the suites look like stage sets. Breakfast is extra.

ⓘ *319, including some suites* 🅿 *(extra)* 🔄 🔟 🔷 *All major cards*

■ Fontana
€€€
PIAZZA DI TREVI 96
TEL 06 678 6113
FAX 06 679 0024
www.hotelfontana-trevi.com
The views of the Fontana di Trevi from the rooftop lounge and breakfast room of this quirky little hotel are breathtaking. Rooms come in all shapes and sizes in the rambling old building, which dates back to the 13th century, when a monastery stood on the site. The location can be sleep-depriving in summer—the noise can go on all night.

ⓘ *25* 🔄 🔟 🔷 *AE, MC, V*

■ La Residenza
€€
VIA EMILIA 22–24
TEL 06 488 0789
FAX 06 485 721
www.hotel-la-residenza.com
At this converted town house conveniently situated near Via Vittorio Veneto, the service is attentive and the rooms are comfortable. The bar, terrace,

and warmly decorated lobbies of this hotel are charming.

① 29, including some junior suites
P Garage ⊟ 🌣 🅰 All major cards

PIAZZA DI SPAGNA TO VILLA BORGHESE

Rome's main shopping district also boasts a variety of interesting and original hotels and restaurants.

🚇 Metro: Spagna, Line A • Bus: 81, 117, 119, 590, 628, 926.

■ Hassler Villa Medici
€€€€€
PIAZZA TRINITÀ DEI MONTI 6
TEL 06 699340
FAX 06 678 9991
www.hotelhasslerroma.com
The hotel's enviable location at the top of the Spanish Steps is matched by elaborate interior design (marble columns and well-upholstered seating) and attentive service. The good-sized rooms are comfortably furnished and have traces of their more than hundred-year history as a hotel. The hotel's panoramic restaurant, Imàgo, has a spectacular view over Rome and serves fine Italian cuisine. Breakfast is extra.

① 95 **P** ⊟ 🌣 🅰 All major cards

■ D'Inghilterra
€€€€€
VIA BOCCA DI LEONE 14
TEL 06 699811
FAX 06 6992 2243
www.royaldemeure.com
Famous for well over a century as one of the best in Rome, this hotel can list Oscar Wilde

among its VIP guests. Antique furnishings tend toward the lugubrious but make for an appropriately historic atmosphere. It's also perfectly placed for the city's most exclusive shopping streets. Breakfast is extra.

① 89 ⊟ 🌣 🅰 All major cards

■ De Russie
€€€€€
VIA BABUINO 9
TEL 06 328881
FAX 06 3288 8888
www.hotelderussie.it
In the heart of the city, between the Spanish Steps and Piazza del Popolo, this hotel is the ultimate in luxury. The guest rooms are spacious and exquisitely decorated. The extensive, terraced gardens are stunning and house the hotel's on-site restaurant, Le Jardin du Russie, a perfect place for a drink or a meal. The menu is devoted to classic Italian cooking with an emphasis on Mediterranean flavors based on olive oil, tomatoes, and garlic.

① 122 plus 33 suites **P** (extra)
⊟ 🌣 🅰 All major cards

■ Art by the Spanish Steps
€€€€
VIA MARGUTTA 56
TEL 06 328711
FAX 06 3600 3995
www.hotelart.it
Color is the theme of this hotel. Previously part of an exclusive private school, the new space incorporates elements of the old with modern minimalism. The guest rooms are reasonably large and highly styled.

① 44 ⊟ 🌣 🅰 All major cards

■ Inn at the Spanish Steps
€€€€
VIA DEI CONDOTTI 85
TEL 06 6992 5657
FAX 06 678 6470
www.atspanishsteps.com
This new, small, family-run luxury residence sits on Rome's famed shopping street, Via dei Condotti, close to the Spanish Steps. Quality and style reign in a discreetly refined atmosphere, with a lovely rooftop terrace for breakfast and aperitifs.

① 24 ⊟ 🌣 🅰 All major cards

■ Forte
€€€
VIA MARGUTTA 61
TEL 06 320 7625
FAX 06 6799 5433
www.hotelforte.com
Located on one of Rome's most charming and peaceful streets, this award-winning hotel offers stylishly decorated rooms in a 17th-century palazzo. Major sites and high-end shopping are only minutes away. Staff can help with information, transfers, and guided tour reservations.

① 18 ⊟ 🌣 🅰 All major cards

■ Locarno
€€€
VIA DELLA PENNA 22
TEL 06 361 0841
FAX 06 321 5249
www.hotellocarno.com
This intriguing art deco hotel is just off Piazza del Popolo. Both the lobbies and guest rooms are tastefully decorated, and in winter there is an open fire in the bar area. It also boasts a lovely roof garden.

① 48 **P** (extra) ⊟ 🌣
🅰 All major cards

HOTELS

TRAVEL ESSENTIALS

■ **Hotel Suisse**
€€
VIA GREGORIANA 54
TEL 06 678 3649
FAX 06 678 1258
www.hotelsuisserome.com
This *pensione* near the top of
the Spanish Steps has been run
by the same family since the
1920s. The light, elegant rooms
have warm wooden flooring
and are decorated with antique
furniture. Some overlook an
internal courtyard, making for a
quiet night's sleep. Friendly staff
can help with booking events
around the city.

🛈 12 🐾 *All major cards*

■ **Parlamento**
€€
VIA DELLE CONVERTITE 5
TEL/FAX 06 6992 1000
www.hotelparlamento.it
A simple, well-run, and
spotlessly clean *pensione,*
where not all rooms have
air-conditioning. Double-glazing
reduces outside noise. Breakfast
is served in the little roof garden
in the summer.

🛈 23 🅿 *Garage* 🔄 🎱 *Extra fee*
🐾 *All major cards*

■ **Teatro di Pompeo**
€€
LARGO DEL PALLARO 8
TEL 06 687 2812
FAX 06 6880 5531
www.hotelteatrodipompeo.it
A small hotel built over the
ruins of a Roman theater, some
of which is still visible. The
rooms are not large but are
tastefully decorated. Street noise
can be a problem.

🛈 13 🚌 *Bus: 116* 🎱
🐾 *All major cards*

PANTHEON TO PIAZZA NAVONA

The true heart of Rome includes
the parliament and senate
buildings, some of the city's
oldest monuments, as well as a
labyrinth of narrow streets and
alleys. It is also home to some
of the city's most established
hotels and restaurants.

🚌 Bus: 40, 46, 62, 63, 64, 70,
81, 87, 116, 119, 492, 628

■ **Grand Hotel
de la Minerve**
€€€€€
PIAZZA DELLA MINERVA 69
TEL 06 695 201
FAX 06 679 4165
**www.grandhoteldela
minerve.com**
Renovated by postmodernist
architect Paolo Portoghesi,
this 17th-century building has
all the comforts of a luxury
hotel, including a beautiful
roof garden, where you can
enjoy a superb view of the
"Eternal City." Guest rooms
are elegantly furnished and of
varying size. Breakfast is extra.
The roof garden restaurant
serves lunch and dinner,
and offers both Italian and
international cuisine.

🛈 135 🅿 *(extra)* 🔄 🎱 📺
🐾 *All major cards*

■ **Raphael**
€€€€
LARGO FEBO 2
TEL 06 682831
FAX 06 687 8993
www.raphaelhotel.com
Just a step away from Piazza
Navona, this hotel is known
for its quiet, luxurious charm
and stunning terrace (closed in

winter) with bar and restaurant.
Guest rooms, though small, are
attractively decorated. Art such
as a Picasso porcelain collection,
fills the lobby. Breakfast is extra.

🛈 50 🚌 *Bus: 70, 81, 87, 116, 280,
492, 628* 🅿 *(extra)* 🔄 🎱 📺
🐾 *All major cards*

■ **Residenza in Farnese**
€€€€
VIA DEL MASCHERONE 59
TEL 06 6821 0980
www.residenzafarneseroma.it
Housed in a converted 14th-
century monastery near Campo
de' Fiori, this quiet, comfortable
hotel has pleasant rooms,
some with frescoed ceilings,
overlooking either the gardens
of the Palazzo Farnese or
Palazzo Spada.

🛈 31 🚌 *Bus: 23, 116, 280*
🔄 🎱 🐾 *All major cards*

■ **Santa Chiara**
€€€€
VIA DI SANTA CHIARA 21
TEL 06 687 2979
FAX 06 687 3144
www.albergosantachiara.com
Located behind the Pantheon,
this hotel is known for its
pleasant, calm atmosphere
and efficient service. Bright
rooms combine function
with comfort.

🛈 100 🅿 *(extra)* 🔄 🎱
🐾 *All major cards*

■ **Due Torri**
€€€
VICOLO DEL LEONETTO 23
TEL 06 6880 6956
FAX 06 686 5442
www.hotelduetorriroma.com
Elegant furnishings and a warm
welcome combine with a
romantic atmosphere to make

this one of the most attractive hotels in its price category. The 19th-century building, on a quiet street near Piazza Navona, used to be the home of bishops and cardinals.

(i) 26 **(F)** *Bus: 70, 81, 87, 116, 280, 492, 628* **P** **⊖** **(S)**
(S) *All major cards*

■ Teatropace 33
€€
VIA DEL TEATRO PACE 33, 00186
TEL 06 687 9075
FAX 06 6819 2364
www.hotelteatropace.com
Opened in 2004, this 17th-century former cardinal's residence offers tastefully appointed bedrooms equipped with modern comforts. Conveniently located 60 feet (18 m) from Piazza Navona.

(i) 23 **(F)** *Bus: 70, 81, 87, 116, 492, 628* **(S)** **(S)** *All major cards*

VATICANO
Much of the solidly respectable residential area around the Vatican dates from the late 19th and early 20th centuries. Some unflashy but high-quality hotels can be found here. With few exceptions, most of the touristy eating places close to the Vatican are best avoided. For public transport, see individual listings.

■ Farnese
€€€
VIA A. FARNESE 30
TEL 06 321 2553
FAX 06 321 5129
www.hotelfarnese.com
A charming choice (and value for money) in the residential Prati area near St. Peter's, connected to the center by the

Metro. Tranquil atmosphere with 17th-century decor and comfortable rooms.

(i) 23 **(F)** *Metro: Lepanto, Line A • Bus: 70, 224, 280, 590* **P** **⊖** **(S)** **(S)** *All major cards*

■ Columbus
€€
VIA DELLA CONCILIAZIONE 33
TEL 06 686 5435
FAX 06 686 4874
www.hotelcolumbus.net
A 15th-century building right in front of St. Peter's is the setting for this aristocratically austere hotel. Guest rooms and bathrooms are functional, but public areas make up with a surfeit of carved stone and frescoed walls.

(i) 92 **(F)** *Bus: 23, 34, 40, 62, 982* **P** **⊖** **(S)** **(S)** *All major cards*

■ Hotel dei Mellini
€€
VIA MUZIO CLEMENTI 81
TEL 06 324 771
FAX 06 3247 7801
www.hotelmellini.com
Spacious rooms with marble bathrooms and a fine roof terrace and bar make this a pleasant and comfortable hotel. It also has great transport links.

(i) 80 **P** *(extra)* **⊖** **(S)**
(S) *All major cards*

■ Sant'Anna
€€
BORGO PIO 133/134
TEL 06 6880 1602
FAX 06 6830 8717
www.santannahotel.net
Located in the shadow of Basilica di San Pietro, this small family-run hotel offers tastefully decorated, comfortable rooms and caring service. Breakfast

is served in a pleasant, inside garden in the summer.

(i) 20 **(F)** *Bus: 23, 34, 40, 62, 280, 982* **P** *(extra)* **⊖** **(S)**
(S) *All major cards*

TRASTEVERE TO GIANICOLO
Visitors and Romans alike come nightly in search of a good time in this lively area "across the Tiber." It has always been packed with bars and restaurants, but recently a number of appealing hotels have also opened.

(F) *Bus: H, 23, 75, 115, 125, 280, 780 • Tram: 3, 8*

■ Donna Camilla Savelli
€€€
VIA GARIBALDI 27
TEL 06 588 861
FAX 06 588 2101
www.hotelsavelli.com
After a remarkable restoration, this 17th-century convent in the heart of Trastevere now operates as a refined hotel. There is a reading room, roof garden, and Internet access.

(i) 78 **P** **⊖** **(S)** **(S)** *All major cards*

■ Hotel Santa Maria
€€€
VICOLO DEL PIEDE 2
TEL 06 589 4626
FAX 06 589 4815
www.htlsantamaria.com
A charming, ground-floor hotel set in the tranquil garden of a 16th-century cloister, only a few minutes from Piazza Santa Maria in Trastevere.

(i) 18 **P** **(S)** **(S)** *All major cards*

HOTELS

■ **San Francesco**

€€€

VIA JACOPADE SETTESOLI 7
TEL 06 5830 0051
FAX 06 5833 3413
www.hotelsanfrancesco.net
Offering pleasant, quiet guest
rooms, this hotel has a breakfast
area facing a 15th-century
cloister and a terrace with a
360-degree panoramic view
over Rome. Very friendly staff.
🅳 24 🅿 (extra) ⮂ 🆂
🆂 All major cards

■ **Villa della Fonte**

€€€

VIA DELLA FONTE D'OLIO 8
TEL 06 580 3797
FAX 06 580 3796
www.villafonte.com
A tiny, welcoming hotel a few
yards from Piazza Santa Maria
in Trastevere. Guest rooms are
comfortable and well-equipped,
and a lovely terrace allows
guests to relax after a busy day.
Breakfast is extra.
🅳 5 🆂 🆂 All major cards

■ **Domus Tiberina**

€€

VIA IN PISCINULA 37
TEL 06 581 3648
www.hoteldomustiberina.it
This hotel, in the heart of
Trastevere near Santa Cecilia
and Tiber Island, has comfortable,
attractively decorated rooms
and a restaurant.
🅳 10 🆂 🆂 All major cards

■ **Hotel Trastevere**

€€

VIA LUCIANO MANARE 24A
TEL 06 581 4713
www.hoteltrastevere.net
This clean and simple hotel has
been recently renovated. All

the rooms are en suite and air-
conditioned, and face the pretty
San Cosimato square.
🅳 9 🆂 🆂 All major cards

■ **Orsa Maggiore**
Women's Hostel

€€

VIA SAN FRANCESCO DI SALES 1
TEL 06 689 3753
www.casainternazionale
delledonne.org/foresteria.htm
Housed in a 16th-century
former convent in Trastevere,
the Orsa Maggiore offers
accommodations for women
only. Completely refurbished
in the building's antique style,
the rooms are simple and look
onto a peaceful courtyard.
Both singles and dormitory
accommodations are available,
and there is a restaurant.
🅳 13 🚍 Bus: H, 23, 75, 115, 125,
271, 280, 780 ⮂ 🆂
🆂 All major cards

THE GHETTO TO TESTACCIO

This green, leafy hill just outside
the center has been one of
Rome's most sought after
residential areas since ancient
times; it now contains some
excellent, tranquil hotels. Many
of the nearest restaurants are
in the popular Testaccio area or
the Ghetto. For public transport,
see individual listings.

■ **Sant'Anselmo**

€€€€

PIAZZA DI SANT'ANSELMO 2
TEL 06 570057
www.aventinohotels.com
Sant'Anselmo's lush garden
shaded with orange trees

on the Aventino makes the
perfect setting for relaxing after
sightseeing. And you can wake
to the singing of birds yet be at
the Foro Romano in minutes.
The lobbies and guest rooms
are attractively decorated.
🅳 46 🚍 Bus: 175, 715
🅿 ⮂ 🆂 🆂 All major cards

■ **Forty Seven**

€€€

VIA LUIGI PETROSELLI 47
TEL 06 678 7816
FAX 06 6919 0726
www.fortysevenhotel.com
Each floor of this new,
centrally located hotel is
dedicated to a 20th-century
Italian artist: Mastroianni,
Greco, Modigliani, Quagliata,
or Guccione. The guest rooms
are large and luminous, many
overlooking the surrounding
monuments. The roof terrace
has good views.
🅳 61 🆂 🆂 Visa

■ **Residence Palazzo**
al Velabro

€€€

VIA DEL VELABRO 16
TEL 06 679 2758
FAX 06 679 3790
www.velabro.it
If you are planing to stay a week
or more this could be a good
choice. Centrally located near
the Palatino and a few steps
from Piazza Bocca della Verità, it
offers quiet, comfortable studio
apartments with kitchenettes,
suitable for two to four people.
Some have wonderful views
from their own terrace.
🅳 35 🚍 Bus: C3, 81, 95, 170,
715, 716, 628 ⮂ 🆂
🆂 All major cards

TRAVEL ESSENTIALS

Yes *Sì*
No *No*
Excuse me (in a crowd or asking for permission) *Permesso*
Excuse me (asking for attention) *Mi scusi*
Hello (before lunch) *Buon giorno,* (after lunch) *Buona sera*
Hi or Bye *Ciao* (very informal)
Please *Per favore*
Thank you *Grazie*
You're welcome *Prego*
Have a good day! *Buona giornata!*
OK *Va bene*
Goodbye *Arrivederci*
Good night *Buona notte*
Sorry *Mi scusi* or *Mi dispiace*
Here *qui*
There *lì*
Today *oggi*
Yesterday *ieri*
Tomorrow *domani*
Now *adesso/ora*
Later *più tardi/dopo*
This morning *stamattina*
This afternoon *questo pomeriggio*
This evening *stasera*
Open *aperto*
Closed *chiuso*
Do you have? *Avete?*
Do you speak English? *Parla inglese?*
I don't understand *Non capisco*
Can you speak more slowly? *Potrebbe parlare più piano?*
Where is...? *Dov' è...?*
Here/there it is (masculine) *Eccolo,* (feminine) *Eccola*
What is your name? *Come si chiama?*
My name is... *Mi chiamo...*
When? *Quando?*
What time is it? *Che ore sono?*
Can you help me? *Mi può aiutare?*

I'd like... *Vorrei...*
How much is it? *Quanto costa?*

MENU READER

Breakfast *la (prima) colazione*
Lunch *il pranzo*
Dinner *la cena*
Appetizer *l'antipasto*
First course *il primo*
Main course *il secondo*
Vegetable, side dish *il contorno*
Dessert *il dessert*
Wine list *la carta dei vini*
The bill *il conto*
I'd like to order *Vorrei ordinare*
Is service included? *Il servizio è incluso?*

Meat

al sangue very rare
appena cotta rare
non troppo cotta medium
ben cotta well-done

l'abbacchio lamb
l'anatra duck
la bistecca beefsteak
il carpaccio finely sliced raw cured beef
il fegato liver
il filetto filet steak
il maiale pork
il manzo beef
misto di carne mixed grill
il pollo chicken
le polpette meatballs
la porchetta cold roast pork
il prosciutto ham, **crudo** raw, **cotto** cooked
straccetti pan-fried strips of beef or veal
il tacchino turkey

Fish

L'alici/acciughe anchovies
l'aragosta/astice lobster
la baccalà salt cod

i calamari squid
le cozze mussels
i gamberetti shrimp
i gamberi prawns
il granchio crab
le ostriche oysters
il salmone salmon
le sarde sardines
la sogliola sole
la spigola bass
il tonno tuna
la trota trout

Vegetables
l'aglio garlic
gli asparagi asparagus
il carciofo artichoke
la carota carrot
la cicoria chicory
la cipolla onion
i fagioli dried beans, usually haricot or borlotti
i fagiolini fresh green beans
i funghi (porcini) mushrooms
l'insalata mista/verde mixed/green salad
la melanzana eggplant
le patate potatoes
le patatine fritte french fries
le patatine potato chips
il peperone bell pepper
i piselli peas
i pomodori tomatoes
il riso rice
gli spinaci spinach

Fruit
l'ananas pineapple
l'arancia orange
le ciliegie cherries
le fragole strawberries
la mela apple
la nocepesca nectarine
la pera pear
la pesca peach
l'uva grapes

TRAVEL ESSENTIALS

INDEX

INDEX

CREDITS

Author
Katie Parla

Additional text by Annabel Howard, Antony Mason, Alice Peebles, Barbara Somogyiova, Joe Yogerst

Picture Credits
t = top; b = bottom, l = left; r = right, m = middle
2-3 Geoff Stringer/Lonely Planet Images; **4** Tony Halliday; **5tr** Stefano Amantini/Atlantide Phototravel/Corbis; **5bl** Tony Halliday; **5mr** Gianluca Figliola Fantini/Shutterstock; **6** Photo Scala, Florence; **9** Tim E. White/Alamy; **12-13** Tony Halliday; **14ml** vvoe/Shutterstock; **14bl** JordiRamisa/iStockphoto; **15t** Tony Halliday; **15b** k.Shulte/www.photolibrary.com; **16** Tony Halliday; **18** Justin Black/Shutterstock; **19,20** Tony Halliday; **21t** Tony Halliday; **21mr** John Kellerman/Alamy; **21br** Giorgio Cosulich/Getty Images; **22** Dennis Marsico/Corbis; **24** Vittorio Zunino Celotto/Getty Images; **25t** Frank Chang/Dreamstime.com; **25m** T.C. Bird; **25b** Oleg Znamenskiy/Shutterstock; **27** Christopher Groenhout/Lonely Planet Images; **28ml** Tony Halliday; **28br** Michael Avory/Shutterstock; **29t** Time Elevator Roma; **29mr** Hermann Dobler/Imagebroker.net/www.photolibrary.com; **30** Guido Baviera/SIME/4Corners; **32** Martin Moos/Lonely Planet Images; **33tm** Tony Halliday **33tr** Just ASC/Shutterstock; **33br** Bob Wickley/Superstock; **35** Giorgio Cosulich/Getty Images; **36-37** Gavin Hellier/White/www.photolibrary.com; **40** Tony Halliday; **42** Juanma Aparicio/Age Fotostock/www.photolibrary.com; **43** Tony Halliday; **45** Pixtal Images/www.photolibrary.com; **47** Peter Erik Forsberg/Age footstock/www.photolibrary.com; **49** Tony

Halliday; **51** Tony Halliday; **52-53** Tony Halliday; **55** René Mattes/Hemis/www.photolibrary.com; **56-57** Tony Halliday; **58l** Tony Halliday; **58r** Gianni Dagli Orti/The Art Archive/Alamy; **59** Tony Halliday; **60** Paul Seheult/Eye Ubiquitous/Corbis; **61** Paolo Cordelli/Lonely Planet Images; **62** Tony Halliday; **65** Sam Bloomberg-Rissman/Alamy; **66** Tony Halliday; **68** Museo Archeologico Nazionale, Naples, Italy/The Bridgeman Art Library; **69** Archaeological Museum Merida Spain/Collection Dagli Orti/The Art Archive; **71** Eric Vandeville/Gamma-Rapho/Getty Images; **72** Will Salter/Lonely Planet Images; **74** Tony Halliday; **75** Alessandro Di Meo, POOL/AP/PA Photos; **77** Tony Halliday; **79** Tony Halliday; **80** Tony Halliday; **82** Massimo Listri/Corbis; **83** Ullsteinbild/TopFoto; **85** Tony Halliday; **86** Tony Halliday; **88tl** Tony Halliday; **88tr** Michael Zegers/Imagebroker.net/www.photolibrary.com; **89r** Tony Halliday; **89l** a123luha/Shutterstock; **91** Christian Handl/Imagebroker.net/www.photolibrary.com; **93** Paolo Cordelli/Lonely Planet Images; **94** Tony Halliday; **96** Andrea Cabibbo/iStockphoto; **97** Tony Halliday; **99** San Rostro/Age footstock/www.photolibrary.com; **101** Dallas and John Heaton/www.photolibrary.com; **102** Fondo Edifii di Culto – Min. dell'Interno/Photo Scala, Florence; **103l** Tony Halliday; **103r** Courtesy of the Ministero Beni e Att.Culturali/Photo Scala, Florence; **104** Tony Halliday; **106** Tony Halliday; **108** Alinari Archives/Corbis; **110** René Mattes/Hemis/www.photolibrary.com; **111** AFP/Getty Images; **113** Godong/Photononstop/www.photolibrary.com; **114** Tony Halliday; **116-117** Tony Halliday; **119** DEA/A.Dagli

Orti/De Agostini Editore; **121** Hedda Gjerpen/iStockphoto; **122** Tony Halliday; **124** Dallas and John Heaton/www.photolibrary.com; **126** Walter Zerla/Age footstock/www.photolibrary.com; **127** Atlantide Phototravel/Corbis; **129** Tony Halliday; **130** deepbluephotographer/Shutterstock; **132t** eclypse78/Shutterstock; **132m** Rostislav Glinsky/Shutterstock; **132b** Tupungato/Shutterstock; **133** Dino/Shutterstock; **134** Tony Halliday; **137** Tony Halliday; **138** Felipe Rodriguez/Alamy; **141** Robert Lehmann/www.photolibrary.com; **142** Galleria degli Uffizi, Florence, Italy/Alinari/The Bridgeman Art Library; **143** Tony Halliday; **145** javarman/Shutterstock; **146** Tony Halliday; **148t** Tony Halliday; **148b** Carole Anne Ferris/Alamy; **149t** Alvaro Leiva/Age footstock/www.photolibrary.com; **149b** maxphotography/iStockphoto; **151** Tony Halliday; **154** Tony Halliday; **156** San Rostro/age footstock/www.photolibrary.com; **157** Tony Halliday; **159** Musacchio & Ianniello; **160** Raimund Kutter/Imagebroker.net/www.photolibrary.com; **162** Alberto Pizzoli/AFP/Getty Images; **163l** Wayne Fogden/Ticket/www.photolibrary.com; **163r** Eugene Mogilnikov/Shutterstock.com; **164** Tony Halliday; **167** Ufficio Stampa Santa Cecilia-Riccardo Musacchio/AP/PA Photos; **169** Elio Lombardo/www.photolibrary.com; **170** Tony Halliday; **173** Paul Raftery/View Pictures/www.photolibrary.com; **174-175** Will Salter/Lonely Planet Images.

Front cover Lovattpics | istockphoto
Back cover Vladimir Mucababic | Shutterstock

Walking Rome

Published by the National Geographic Society

John M. Fahey, Jr., *Chairman of the Board
and Chief Executive Officer*
Timothy T. Kelly, *President*
Declan Moore, *Executive Vice President;
President, Publishing*
Melina Gerosa Bellows, *Executive Vice President,
Chief Creative Officer, Books, Kids, and Family*

Prepared by the Book Division

Barbara Brownell Grogan, *Vice President and Editor in Chief*
Jonathan Halling, *Design Director, Books and
Children's Publishing*
Marianne R. Koszorus, *Design Director, Books*
Barbara A. Noe, *Senior Editor*
Carl Mehler, *Director of Maps*
Lawrence M. Porges, *Project Editor*
Marty Ittner, *Design Consultant*
Whitney Jones, Lise Sajewski, Mary Stephanos,
Contributors
R. Gary Colbert, *Production Director*
Mike Horenstein, *Production Manager*
Jennifer A. Thornton, *Managing Editor*
Meredith C. Wilcox, *Administrative Director, Illustrations*

Travel Publications

Keith Bellows, *Vice President and Editor in Chief*
Jerry Sealy, *Director of Design*

Manufacturing and Quality Management

Christopher A. Liedel, *Chief Financial Officer*
Phillip L. Schlosser, *Senior Vice President*
Chris Brown, *Technical Director*
Nicole Elliott, *Manager*
Rachel Faulise, *Manager*
Robert L. Barr, *Manager*

Created by Toucan Books Ltd

Ellen Dupont, *Editorial Director*
Alice Peebles, *Senior Editor*
Peter Clubb, Jane Hutchings, Andrew Kerr-Jarrett,
Anna Southgate, *Editors*
Leah Germann, *Designer*
Christine Vincent, *Picture Manager*
Sharon Southren, *Picture Researcher*
Merritt Cartographic, *Maps*
Beth Landis Hester, *Proofreader*
Marie Lorimer, *Indexer*

CREDITS

The National Geographic Society is one of the world's
largest nonprofit scientific and educational organizations.
Founded in 1888 to "increase and diffuse geographic
knowledge," the Society works to inspire people to care
about the planet. National Geographic reflects the world
through its magazines, television programs, films, music and
radio, books, DVDs, maps, exhibitions, live events, school
publishing programs, interactive media and merchandise.
National Geographic magazine, the Society's official journal,
published in English and 33 local-language editions, is read
by more than 40 million people each month. The National
Geographic Channel reaches 370 million households
in 34 languages in 168 countries. National Geographic
Digital Media receives more than 15 million visitors a
month. National Geographic has funded more than
9,600 scientific research, conservation and exploration
projects and supports an education program promoting
geography literacy. For more information, visit www.
nationalgeographic.com.

For more information, please call 1-800-NGS LINE
(647-5463) or write to the following address:

National Geographic Society
1145 17th Street N.W.
Washington, D.C. 20036-4688 U.S.A.

For information about special discounts for bulk purchases,
please contact National Geographic Books Special Sales:
ngspecsales@ngs.org

For rights or permissions inquiries, please contact National
Geographic Books Subsidiary Rights: ngbookrights@ngs.org

ISBN: 978-1-4262-0872-0

Copyright © 2012 National Geographic Society
All rights reserved. Reproduction of the whole or any
part of the contents without written permission from the
publisher is prohibited.

Printed in Italy

11/MV/1

The information in this book has been carefully checked and is, to the best
of our knowledge, accurate as of press time. It's always advisable to call
ahead, however, as details are subject to change. The National Geographic
Society cannot be responsible for any changes, or for errors or omissions.